THE DARWEN COUNTY HISTORY SERIES

A History of
KENT

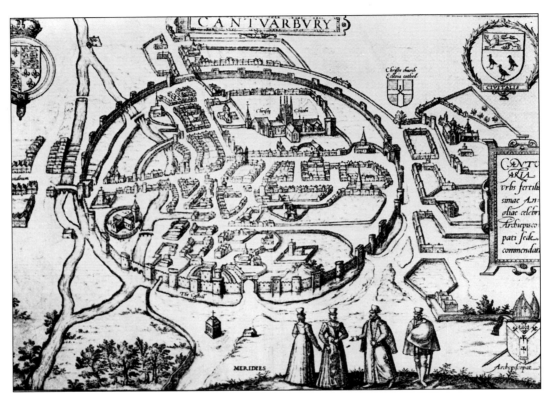

Hoefnagel's map of Canterbury is thought to date from c.1570

**THE DARWEN COUNTY
HISTORY SERIES**

A History of
KENT

Frank W. Jessup

Phillimore

1995

Published by
PHILLIMORE & CO. LTD.
Shopwyke Manor Barn, Chichester, West Sussex

First published 1974
Reprinted 1978
Revised Edition 1995

© J.H. Jessup, 1995

ISBN 0 85033 916 2

Printed and bound in Great Britain by
BUTLER & TANNER LTD.
Frome, Somerset

Contents

Kentish waggon
(after a drawing by
T. Hennell)

List of Illustrations

Frontispiece: Hoefnagel's map of Canterbury

List of Colour Plates

Illustration Acknowledgements

The following have given their permission to reproduce illustrations: the Centre for Kentish Studies, nos. 44, 67, 109, 119, 120, 130 and 133; the Controller of Her Majesty's Stationery Office, no. 3; Kent County Council, no. 17 (the charter of King Wihtred's is held in the Kent Archives Office). No. 77 is reproduced from *Timber and Brick Building in Kent* (Phillimore & Co. Ltd., 1971). The portrait of William Lambarde, no. 100, is taken from *William Lambarde, Elizabethan Antiquary, 1536-1601* (Phillimore & Co. Ltd., 1973). Illustrations 128-9 are by the author. Ivan Green has kindly supplied the remainder of the photographs.

The line drawings are by Alison Crawford, Anne Krämer and Carole Machin, whilst the maps have been drawn by Aylwin Sampson and Thomas Bernard.

Cranbrook Mill

From the Preface to the First Edition

Scylla and Charybdis await the writer of a county history. On the one hand he may fall into the danger of writing of what is essentially national history, illustrated with a number of, more or less, apt examples drawn from the county; or, on the other hand, his history may become a disconnected chronicle of, literally insignificant, local events. These are difficulties that arise from the fact that counties are not natural units, with an independent existence and a continuous history. In this respect the historian of Kent has a comparatively easy task, for not only is the county (as I believe) richer in history than any other in England, but also its peninsular configuration gives it something of a natural unity. It acquired an identity and an individuality earlier than almost any other part of the country, and in some ways it has managed to retain them, in spite of its nearness to the capital, and in spite of it being the highway to and from the Continent.

Since to write a continuous narrative county history is impossible, it must take the form of a series of accounts of the most important periods and topics. But in deciding which periods and topics are abundant and ready to hand, the author is bound to be influenced by his own personal interests. Moreover, for some subjects the materials are abundant and ready to hand, for others they are scanty and hard to come by. For these reasons no county history is likely to present an elegantly balanced pattern, and I am conscious of shortcomings in this book, not least of omission.

In so short a book there is little room for the introduction of original material. A few things are included which have not, I think, previously appeared in print, but in the main I have stood on other men's shoulders (or if, occasionally and inadvertently, on their toes, I apologise).

To the authors of all those works I am deeply indebted, as I am to also to many friends for help and advice.

1

Before the Romans

From the South Foreland to Cap Gris Nez is a distance of only 21 miles. On a clear day the chalk cliffs of the French coast can easily be seen from the opposing cliffs on the Kent shore of the Strait of Dover. The chalk cliffs are only one of the natural features to be found on both sides of the Channel; the countryside of East Kent and that of northern France have much in common, nor is this surprising, for until about eight thousand years ago the territory that we now know as Kent formed a continuous land-mass with the continent of Europe, and our North Downs, which fall so abruptly into the sea between Dover and Folkestone, were part of a great range of chalk hills which stretched from Salisbury Plain eastwards into Flanders. Thus there was no physical obstacle to migration into these lands, which formed merely a north-western peninsula to the mainland of Europe. Moreover, men had not yet learnt the art of agriculture, so crop-growing did not root them to a particular locality. They wandered wherever game and vegetable foods were plentiful, water was easily accessible and the climate was not too rigorous. It was through Kent, which formed the neck of the peninsula, that the migrants, pressing north-westward from the heart of Europe, passed into Britain.

The slow sinking of the land in relation to the sea resulted in the isthmus gradually becoming narrower, until finally the sea broke through, the land-bridge was severed, and the waters of the North Sea and the English Channel flowed together. It has been estimated that this cataclysmic change took place somewhere about the year 6,000 B.C. The strait which was thus formed between Britain and Europe was not an insurmountable obstacle but it must have meant that migration into Britain ceased to be the result of casual wandering and that it now became an operation deliberately to be embarked upon.

The south-east corner of Britain, which later acquired the name of Kent, was in no sense a separate unit in prehistoric times. Like the rest of Britain it was very sparsely populated, and its early inhabitants, in common with those of Western Europe generally, achieved but a low standard of culture; they used implements made of flint, not having discovered how to work metal; they did not know how to make pottery; they were not farmers, neither raising crops nor keeping livestock. Somewhere about the year 2,000 B.C. (this must be regarded as a very approximate date) there are signs that further migrations led to an advance of civilisation in the lowland area of Britain which was so marked that

1 *Palaeolithic flint implement*

15

it has been called the Neolithic Revolution. The newcomers were still ignorant of the use of metals, but they showed great skill in making flint implements, they cultivated the land and kept herds of cattle, they made pottery, rough but nevertheless serviceable, and some of them raised huge stone monuments, known as megaliths, which have never ceased to be a source of awe and wonder to subsequent generations.

The most impressive Kentish relics of the Neolithic Age are the megaliths of the Medway Valley—Kits Coty, the Countless Stones, Coldrum and the Addington Stones amongst them. They are built of local sarsen stone, but all except Kits Coty, whose three upright stones and capstone remain, have collapsed into a meaningless jumble. Originally these megaliths were associated with long barrows, earthen mounds perhaps 200 ft. long, 30 ft. wide and 15 ft. high, which were erected as communal graves, or possibly sometimes for a single distinguished chieftain. The Kits Coty stones formed a false doorway at one end of a long barrow, all trace of which has now disappeared through constant ploughing, although two hundred and fifty years ago the outlines of it could still be made out on the surface of the field, and part of it can even now be seen from the air. The purpose of the false doorway is not certainly known; perhaps it was to mislead marauders, perhaps to prevent spirits of the dead emerging from their grave to haunt the living.

2 Kits Coty as it appeared at the end of the 18th century

The men who built the long barrows of the Medway Valley and the one in the Stour Valley at Chilham, called Juliberrie's Grave, belonged to the same general civilisation as those who erected parts of the great monument of

Stonehenge. Originating in the lands that border the north side of the Mediterranean, they made their way up the west coast of the Iberian peninsula and of France across the English Channel into the south of Britain, and by sea into Wales, Ireland, the Hebrides, and Scotland and into Scandinavia and North Germany. It was essentially a water-borne civilisation. Megalithic remains in eastern England generally are scanty, and it is significant that the Kentish megaliths all lie near a river. Probably the people who constructed them did not come directly from the Mediterranean but settled first on the east side of the North Sea, before later migrating to Britain.

Another migration into Kent took place at about the same time as that of the megalith-builders. These other newcomers crossed the Channel from France and the Low Countries into south and east Britain. In spite of these immigrations, much of the land nevertheless remained unoccupied. Parts of the region, such as the Weald, and the long northern dip-slope of the Downs, carried a dense forest on the clay, and these areas naturally were avoided, remaining unsettled or but sparsely populated until almost the end of the Middle Ages. The areas chiefly favoured by Neolithic man, as is evident from the finds of flint implements and pottery, were: Thanet; the Dour Valley, running inland from Dover, and the foot of the Downs behind Folkestone; and the valleys of the Stour, Medway, Darent and Cray, especially where, as at Aylesford and Crayford, patches of gravel afforded convenient crossings and well-drained areas for settlement.

The second millennium B.C. was an era of great folk-movements in Europe, and it was with one of these, perhaps about 1,800 B.C., that the idea of metal-working was introduced into southern Britain. The people who brought this knowledge with them (sometimes called *Beaker folk*, from the shape of a certain type of pot which is frequently found in their graves) came in the main from Holland and the Rhineland, whence they crossed to Britain, making a series of landings in the river estuaries along the east coast. They themselves were not, at the time of their migration, workers of metal, and the rather simple bronze tools which they brought with them had been acquired in the course of trade. Centuries passed before the Bronze Age people attained the technical ability to make, and had the trading connections to import, such fine bronze swords as those found at Bromley, Aylesford and Chatham, or the socketed axes which are typical of the best work of the Bronze Age. Finds of Bronze Age weapons, tools, pottery and trinkets have been made at many places in Kent. The stock-in-trade of an itinerant bronze-worker found at Minster-in-Thanet contained no fewer than 140 items, including axes, swords, spear-heads, knives, a sickle and a hammer, and a smaller hoard was discovered on the foreshore at Birchington. That it was a period of prosperity is evidenced by the heavy gold ornaments, belonging to the Bronze Age and probably imported from Ireland, which have been found at Bexley, Faversham, Canterbury, Dover, Little Chart, Aylesford and elsewhere in the county.

Bronze, which slowly ousted the use of flint, in its turn gave way before the use of iron, a harder and more serviceable metal. Iron-working was probably introduced into Britain by people from the Continent somewhere about the year

3 *Bronze-Age sword and spear*

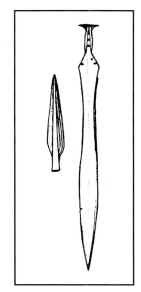

500 B.C. but the new material did not immediately displace the use of bronze. No doubt the use of bronze and of iron went on side-by-side for generations. No doubt, too, the men of the Early Iron Age and of the Bronze Age, as Neolithic men before them, used wood, possibly hardened by fire, for making tools which modern man would fashion from iron or steel, but save in exceptionally favourable conditions wood perishes, and few or no examples of such implements have survived. Pottery-sherds on the other hand are almost imperishable, and Early Iron Age pottery has been found at many places in Kent, the most remarkable discoveries being the urn-fields, or cemeteries, at Aylesford and at Swarling. Most of the other finds of pottery have been on the coast, from Reculver round to Folkestone, in the Stour Valley as far up as Wye, and in the Medway Valley. Hoards of gold coins of this period were found at Higham and Westerham, the coins in each case being inside a hollow flint, evidently used as a money-box. Towards the end of the Early Iron Age coins began to be minted

4 A bronze copy of a fine late Bronze-Age gold torc discovered in Dover in 1878.

in Kent, inscribed with the name of the local ruler.

But far more impressive than pottery-sherds or crudely-minted coins are the great Iron Age hill-top camps at Oldbury, near Ightham, at Keston, and at Bigbury, two miles west of Canterbury. These camps are enclosed by earth ramparts, which at Oldbury were strengthened in places with masonry work, although this reinforcement did not take place until a hundred years or so after the original construction of the camp. Oldbury is huge, the area enclosed being over 120 acres: Bigbury is about a third as large. The comparatively low ramparts at Bigbury could never have been of much defensive value, and it is possible that they were thrown up hurriedly at the time of Julius Caesar's incursions into Britain in 55 and 54 B.C. The Oldbury camp, on the other hand, was built as a stronghold, probably somewhere about the period 80-60 B.C. There are other Iron-Age camps in Kent, for example, at Nettlestead and Squerryes, Westerham, but none of them is so immense and so impressive as Oldbury.

Why did the men of West Kent undertake the enormous labour which the construction of Oldbury camp involved? The answer seems to be that soon after the opening of the first century B.C. fresh bands of invaders began to cross the North Sea, probably from the Low Countries, and to settle in East Kent and elsewhere in Britain. They belonged to the people known as the Belgae, whom Julius Caesar encountered in his Gallic War. Pressing westward from their early settlements in the eastern part of the county, or south-eastward from the territories which they occupied north of the Thames, they would come into contact, and perhaps conflict, with the people dwelling on the west side of the Medway. It seems likely that Oldbury was constructed as a defence against these invaders. However, in the end, although perhaps not until after the middle of the century and after the time of Caesar's expeditions across the Channel, the Belgae prevailed, spreading themselves across the lowland region of Britain.

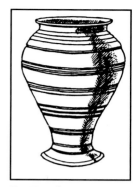

5 *Urn from Iron-Age cemetery, Swarling.*

Caesar's expeditions, or reconnaissances, were not an attempt to conquer Britain, but an extension of his war of conquest and pacification in Gaul. He himself says that he undertook the expeditions to punish the Britons who had been aiding the Gauls in their resistance against the might of Rome. This was no more, in all probability, than a colourful excuse to justify an undertaking to which he was prompted by natural curiosity and by desire of further glory. The crossing in 55 B.C. was made from the French coast near to where the town of Boulogne now stands, with two legions. Their landing in the haven of the River Dour was opposed by the Britons who, says Caesar, lined the cliffs in warlike array, so the Romans sailed along the coast until they could force a landing on the flatter shore at Deal. The Britons soon sued for peace, and although, when Caesar was embarrassed by a high tide which damaged his fleet, they took the opportunity to reopen hostilities, the Roman military power again quickly showed its superiority and for a second time the Britons submitted. After a campaign lasting only a few days, Caesar withdrew to Gaul before the autumn set in, requiring the Britons to send hostages to him and determining to return in the following year.

In 54 B.C. the invading army was a much more formidable force, consisting as it did of five legions and 2,000 Gallic horse, ferried across the Channel in 600 transports. They landed in the same place as before and quickly marched away inland after having established a base camp near the coast. Twelve miles inland the Romans found their crossing of the Stour opposed by the Britons, who probably were occupying the camp on the hill-top at Bigbury, overlooking the river. Again the Britons gave way before the organised and skilfully-led legions, and again, as in the previous year, Caesar was obliged to return to his base camp near the Deal shore because his ships had been damaged in a great storm. Having spent 10 days, which he could ill afford, in re-establishing his base, he resumed the advance into the interior of the country, crossing the Medway, forcing the passage of the Thames (probably somewhere near Brentford) and destroying the capital of Cassivellaunus, the king of the British tribes north of the Thames. Thus Caesar's second expedition drew to an end, not having achieved all that he had hoped of it, but with more positive results than he had achieved the year before.

Caesar wrote the seven books of his Gallic Wars not to help 20th-century historians, nor even to torment 20th-century schoolboys, but to justify his conduct of the campaigns in Gaul and the neighbouring territories, and to record his skill and courage as a soldier. In a word, they were propaganda in the Caesarean cause, and we cannot expect from them any full or objective account of the British tribes with whom he came into contact. Nevertheless, he

6 *Bigbury hill fort, to the west of Canterbury, after scrub had been cleared away*

gives a certain amount of information about them and in particular says that of all the Britons (a statement obviously based upon hearsay, since his first-hand acquaintance with Britain was limited to the south-east corner) 'by far the most civilised are those who inhabit *Cantium*, which is an entirely maritime region, nor do they differ from the Gallic custom'. In the course of trade, the men of Kent were indeed in frequent contact with Gaul and the north-west part of the continent. Their coinage, their stylish pottery, their ability to construct great camps like Oldbury and Bigbury and the degree of political organisation which their construction implies, their use of war-chariots, and the advances which they made in agriculture, show that they were anything but a race of naked, woad-dyed, savages. Some of them had but recently migrated from the Belgic territories on the Continent, bringing with them a mixture of Celtic and Teutonic cultures. The migration was not halted by Caesar's expeditions, and probably continued for another fifty years or so.

About the languages of these early men of Kent and Kentish men it is impossible to say much with certainty. It is generally thought that they used different forms of the Celtic languages, ancestral to Welsh, but Caesar's comments about the Belgae seem to suggest that their tongue may have been related to those of the Germanic family of languages. They have left us no books and no written records from which we can judge. All that remain of their language, or languages, are a few place-names, such as the name Kent itself; the names of the rivers Thames, Medway, Darent, Dour, Stour and Cray; and the names Thanet, Lympne and Reculver. In themselves they give no clue to the character and manner of life of the men whom Caesar encountered, and recorded to posterity as the most civilised of all the Britons, but the fact that names which are still in use go back to the old British language or languages underlines the continuity of Kentish history for over two thousand years.

2

Romano-British Kent

When Caesar withdrew at the end of the campaigning season in 54 B.C. it is very probable that he meant to return the following year, or soon after, to undertake the conquest of Britain in earnest. However, matters elsewhere in the Empire then engaged his attention, especially a series of rebellions in Gaul, and neither Caesar nor his immediate successors could find time or opportunity to return to the British affair begun in 55 and 54 B.C.

This did not mean that contact between Britain and the Continent was broken off. Of direct contact with Rome there was little or none; the defeated Cassivellaunus had promised to pay a stated annual tribute to Rome and perhaps he may have done so for a few years, although that is uncertain. It was not directly with distant Rome but with the highly civilised Belgae of Romanised Gaul that south-east Britain was in close contact. Some Belgic chieftains held sway over tribes on both sides of the English Channel; there was a steady trade across the Strait of Dover, Britain exporting corn, cattle, gold, silver, iron, hides, slaves and hunting-dogs, and importing such luxury goods as wine and oil, bronze furniture, finer pottery than the Britons themselves could make, jewellery, silver table-ware and glass-ware. The coins of the British kings at this period show how much they were under the influence of Gaul, and so, indirectly, of Rome.

7 *Second-century bust, Lullingstone Roman villa.*

Although it was almost a hundred years before the Romans returned to these shores the conquest of Britain was a project that had merely been postponed, not abandoned. At last, in A.D.43 the Emperor Claudius, mistrusting the increasingly anti-Roman attitude of the British leaders and judging that conditions in other parts of the Empire, and especially in Gaul, were now quiet enough for him to embark safely upon a large military expedition, despatched Aulus Plautius with some 40,000 men to undertake the conquest of Britain. They sailed from Boulogne in three divisions, made for the Kentish coast, and landed at Richborough, with perhaps diversionary landings elsewhere. The earthen banks which they threw up to protect their base-camp at Richborough can still be seen within the great masonry walls of the later Roman fort.

At this point it is necessary to digress for a moment to give some description of the Kentish coast as it existed 2,000 years ago. To say that the 'Romans landed at Richborough', that is at a point which is now two miles from the sea, obviously calls for some explanation. The map on page 25 gives some idea of the changes

8   An aerial view of Richborough Castle

9   A section of Richborough's surviving late third-century walls, said to be the best preserved in the country

that have taken place in the coastline since the time of Caesar and Claudius. Thanet was an island, cut off from the mainland by an arm of the sea which slowly silted up, but which remained navigable until the Middle Ages, and was known as the River Wantsum; the coastline of the Thames estuary near Reculver was some distance farther north of its present position; Richborough (*Rutupiae* to give it its old name) was an island in the Wantsum; the great triangle of Romney Marsh and Walland Marsh had not yet been formed (Ebony, meaning *Ebba's* island; Oxney, the isle of oxen; and Midley, middle island, perpetuate in their names the conditions that existed before the Marsh became firm land); Hythe was a coastal harbour; below the hill at Lympne was a harbour on an inlet of the sea; the haven of Dover was inland from the present sea-front on the site of the modern Market Square; and the River Swale was probably twice its present width.

The Roman landing at Richborough was unopposed. The Britons were anything but a homogeneous, united nation and although Cunobelinus (Shakespeare's *Cymbeline*) had enlarged his Belgic kingdom, which was originally limited to the area north of the Thames, by bringing south-east Britain under his sway, the Kentish tribes were still semi-independent. To organise an effective resistance to the invaders was beyond the capacity of Cunobelinus's less able sons, Caractacus and Togodumnus, who succeeded him. Separately they raised armies and hastened into east Kent, but they hastened only to their own defeat, and Plautius became master of Kent east of the Medway. A more serious attempt to stem the Roman advance was made on the line of the Medway, somewhere about Rochester. The fact that the battle lasted two days, most unusual in warfare of that period, shows how fierce a resistance was offered, but by the end of the second day the Britons were streaming westward in defeat. Plautius, in pursuit of the retreating Britons, crossed the Thames at London, and Kent saw no more of the fighting. Within a few years the Romans had brought all the lowland part of Britain under their control, but the attempt to subjugate the northern and western highlands was a long-drawn-out and never entirely successful operation. Thus the army's main pre-occupation was not in the south-east but in the west and north, where it has left such memorials of its power as Hadrian's Wall, and the great legionary forts of Caerleon, Chester and York.

The Roman occupation lasted for a long time, not far short of 400 years. Looking at the period in retrospect we may, unless we are on our guard, endow it with a uniformity which it did not possess. The fortunes of the Roman Empire fluctuated and the province of Britain had its ups and downs no less than the rest. What was true of one century was not necessarily true of the next, and what held good for one part of the country did not necessarily apply to the

10 *The Pharos in the grounds of Dover Castle was a guide beacon for Roman mariners*

11 *Roman figurine from Reculver*

remainder. The British occupation of India lasted only half as long as the Roman occupation of these islands; if we remember how great were the differences which divided the India of Clive from the India of Gandhi and Lord Mountbatten, we shall be less likely to make the mistake of thinking of the Roman era in Britain as possessing a greater homogeneity than it really had.

Into part of Britain the Romans introduced their own system of provincial government, but elsewhere they followed their customary practice of using native chieftains through and by whom the business of government was performed. Near or on the site of the old tribal capitals new Roman cities were built. Thus Roman Canterbury came into existence, possibly supplanting a former tribal capital at nearby Bigbury. Canterbury became an important settlement because it was the junction of the roads which led from the ports of *Rutupiae* (Richborough), *Dubris* (Dover) and *Lemanis* (Lympne) to London and beyond. The modern roads from Canterbury to Sandwich, Dover and Lympne follow over much of their length the lines of the Roman roads, and are still remarkable for their straightness. It was only where there was some serious obstacle, such as the scarp of the Downs above Stanford, that the Roman road deviated from the most direct route. Westward from Canterbury ran the road which much later came to be known as Watling Street, climbing up over the edge of Blean Forest and thence making its way to Rochester in an almost perfectly straight line. Across the Medway at Rochester the Romans built a bridge, supported on wooden piles which were rediscovered in the 19th century, and on the west side of the river the road was carried on a causeway across the marsh to the foot of Strood hill (the name *Strood* is significant, for it means marshy land overgrown with brushwood). From there the road runs in an almost direct line to London, except for slight changes of direction at Cobham woods and at Swanscombe hill.

These were the main roads that the Romans made. They were solid, hard roads, 12 ft. or more in width, and so strongly constructed that they remained in use as the main routes for hundreds of years after the Romans had departed, and were such conspicuous features of the landscape that later they were often adopted as parish boundaries and still serve as such. The purpose of these roads is obvious, to provide communication between London, already a great town and the centre of the road system in Britain, and the ports which were the link with the Continent and distant Rome. Without such a system of communications and roads along which, if the need arose, military forces could speedily be moved, the Empire would never have held together. And besides armies, through these Kentish ports and along these arterial highways travelled merchants and traders engaged in the extensive and profitable import and export business.

Other less important roads also existed, of more commercial than military significance. Some of these roads were constructed to link thickly-settled areas, such as the Medway Valley, with Watling Street. One road, running southward from Rochester and Maidstone, crossed the Weald to Hastings and the Sussex iron-working district; another left that road at a point south of Maidstone and passed eastward along the line of the greensand hills to Lympne; another ran south-westward from Canterbury, over Godmersham Downs, through Ashford,

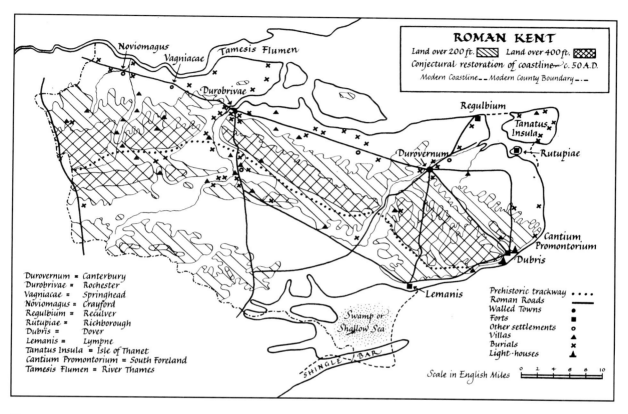

The following abbreviations appear on the map:

Durovernum = Canterbury
Durobrivae = Rochester
Vagniacae = Springhead
Noviomagus = Crayford
Regulbium = Reculver
Rutupiae = Richborough
Dubris = Dover
Lemanis = Lympne
Tanatus Insula = Isle of Thanet
Cantium Promontorium = South Foreland
Tamesis Flumen = River Thames

Tenterden and Benenden to the iron-working district; shorter roads connected Reculver with Canterbury, Lympne with Dover, and Dover with Richborough. And, in addition to the Roman roads, the prehistoric trackways, such as the so-called Pilgrims' Way, no doubt continued in use at least in part, following as they did the most favourable contour line and avoiding the heavy-clays.

Canterbury, Rochester and Dover were Roman towns, of which Canterbury was the largest, yet not to be compared in size with such towns as London, Verulamium, Cirencester, Silchester or Colchester. Canterbury and Rochester, some parts of the Roman walls of which are still visible, mark prominent river-crossings. Dover was a port, and opportunities for excavation in the course of new road construction near the centre of the town during 1971 revealed the existence of a Roman fort of remarkable size and strength. Some of its rooms reached the same high standard of civilised decoration as houses in Italy itself, and there is little doubt that this important fort was the headquarters of the Roman fleet based in Britain. In other parts of Kent, notably along the line of Watling Street at Ospringe and Milton Regis, and, west of the Medway, at Springhead and Dartford; in the Medway Valley from Burham to Wateringbury; and in the Darent Valley, Romanised settlements were numerous and close together, but none of these areas—apart from Springhead, perhaps—could properly be called a town.

12   Map   showing Roman   occupation   in Kent

13 Christian symbol, Lullingstone Roman villa

Country life in Romano-British Kent, as elsewhere in Britain, was organised on a different basis from town life. The characteristic feature of the countryside was the *villa*, of which more than fifty examples are known in Kent; four of the finest are those at Lullingstone, Eccles, Folkestone and Darenth. *Villa* is apt to be a misleading term; these Roman country houses must be thought of more in terms of the medieval manor house, surrounded by its estate of farm-lands, than as comparable with a Renaissance Italian villa, or still less with the sort of building that now goes by that name. Not all villas, in fact, were farmhouses. The large villa on the East Cliff at Folkestone may or may not have been an official residence of the admiral in command of the Roman fleet in Britain, but it can scarcely have been the centre of an agricultural estate. The even larger villa at Darenth was apparently used for fulling cloth, an indication that the weaving of local wool into cloth was an active industry in Kent. Other industries were the making of tiles at Plaxtol, of pottery at many places, including Upchurch which has given its name to a widely found variety of pottery, the quarrying of stone near Maidstone and Lympne, and, near the Sussex border, the smelting and forging of iron-ore. Agriculture, however, as throughout Kent's history, was the most important industry, especially the growing of corn and even as far back as the first century A.D. Kent farmers had learnt sufficient of the art of agriculture to know the advantages of dressing the heavier clay-lands with marl or chalk which was dug for that purpose.

Throughout Britain, and indeed throughout the Empire, town-life was in decay by the end of the third century. The reasons for the decline are obscure, and it is the more puzzling that this was the period when the villa system was at its zenith. Whatever the explanation, there is no gainsaying the evidence.

The fourth century saw the beginning of Britain's time of troubles. Through internal dissension and the aggressions of barbarians from without, the Empire had been so weakened that it was no longer in a position to control events in its outermost provinces. The Picts of North Britain and the Irish, two peoples who had never submitted to Roman dominion, resumed their raids, and even came as far south as Kent. Meanwhile the barbarians from across the North Sea began to harry the maritime countryside and it was against the menace of the Saxon and Frankish pirates that about the year 300 a series of 11 great forts were built at strategic points along the coast from the Wash to the Isle of Wight. No fewer than four of them were in Kent—Reculver, Richborough, Dover and Lympne. A fleet to guard Britain had been in existence from the first century A.D., as we know from the many tiles that have been discovered at Folkestone, Dover, Lympne and elsewhere stamped with the letters CL BR, i.e. *Classis Britannica*, the Britannic fleet. In the fourth century the forts were associated with the fleet and an officer called the Count of the Saxon Shore was appointed to take charge of coastal defence by land and by sea.

Of the four Kentish forts the northern part of Reculver has been washed away by the sea, but the south, and parts of the east and west walls remain, now enclosing the ruins of a Saxon church founded in the seventh century; Stutfall Castle at Lympne has collapsed down the hillside, and is represented only by scattered blocks of fallen masonry; the remains of the great fort at

Dover, which stood on the floor of the valley, not on the site of the existing Dover Castle, have only recently been rediscovered; Richborough survives as an impressive ruin, with huge walls 10 to 12 ft. thick and in places 25 ft. high which stand up above the level of the marsh as a startling visual reminder of the might of Rome.

Nevertheless these defences could not, in the end, protect Britain from invasion by the Saxons and the Franks. By the beginning of the fifth century the Empire was under attack on many fronts, and Rome herself was in danger. Some troops were withdrawn from Britain and the chain of military command broke down. The Emperor could only advise the Britons to shift for themselves, and although there may have been a partial Roman re-occupation for a few years the link with Rome, by about A.D. 425, had finally been severed.

What were the effects of the Roman occupation on Britain, and especially on this south-eastern corner of the province, *Cantium*? Judging from the number of coins, from the quality of the pottery which has been discovered, from the excellent glassware which was imported, and from the number of great *amphorae* for wine and oil, brought from the Mediterranean, it was a time of material prosperity based partly on agriculture, partly on Kent's position across the main route from London to Gaul and Rome. The roads which the Romans built left a permanent mark on the face of the countryside. The larger farmers inhabiting their villas, centrally heated and with a sometimes elaborate system of bathhouses, lived a life of considerable comfort. In Canterbury there was a theatre as well as public baths for the delectation of the citizens. Industry was scattered; in a few centres it at tained a level of some importance. The upper classes spoke Latin, and so also to some extent did the artisans, as we know from the comments which builders sometimes scrawled, in Latin, on the buildings on which they were working, and from the tiles from the Plaxtol villa which bear the maker's advertising slogan, spelled out in Latin.

In matters of art the Romans contributed little. In religion it was otherwise. The worship of the British local gods was not forbidden—Romano-Celtic temples at Richborough and Worth are evidence of such toleration, but the army introduced the cults of Jupiter, Mars and Mercury, and eastern religions from Egypt, Syria and Asia. Christianity seems to have reached Britain not later than the year A.D. 200, and made steady progress during the third century. If Christian churches were built in this period, none has survived. However, within the last few years the excavation of the Roman villa at Lullingstone has revealed that the walls of one room were once painted with Christian symbols and pictures, and probably what was true of one villa was true also of some of the others.

We must now turn to the question of what happened to this civilisation when the Romans finally left these islands.

3

Saxon Kent

Long as was the duration of the Roman occupation, the period from the departure of the Romans to the Norman Conquest was longer still, as long as the period which divides our day from the Battle of Crécy and the Black Death. So long a span of time was bound to bring important changes, and Saxon Kent of the 11th century differed in many respects from Saxon Kent of the fifth.

The Saxons and the Franks, as we have already seen, were making raids on the south and east coasts of Britain as early as the end of the third century. After the Roman withdrawal a period of confusion set in. The Britons did not constitute an organised nation, united in defence against the threatened raids from across the North Sea. Internally there was dissension, with pro-Roman and anti-Roman parties, and the situation was made more confused by incursions of the Picts from Scotland. Tradition has it that in A.D. 449 Vortigern, who was king in Kent, sought the help of Hengist and Horsa, two Jutish leaders, in protecting his kingdom against attack, promising them the Isle of Thanet as a reward for their assistance. It is likely that this was by no means the first occasion on which a Romanised British leader had called in the aid of mercenaries from the Continent. Many of the details of the traditional Hengist and Horsa story are patently fictitious, but in outline it is probably true. What is certain is that the newcomers, having established themselves in east Kent, were followed across the sea by others belonging to the same people.

It has been customary since Bede wrote his *Ecclesiastical History* in 731 to refer to these invaders of Kent as Jutes, distinguishing them from the Angles who settled the area we know as East Anglia, and from the Saxons, who have left a permanent memorial of themselves in the territorial names Essex (East Saxons), Sussex (South Saxons), Middlesex (Middle Saxons) and Wessex (West Saxons). But the origin of the 'Jutes' remains a debatable question. Probably there will always be some uncertainty about them for the fifth century was a period of large-scale folk migrations on the Continent, and it is unlikely that they were a closely-knit people or that they came from a single district of Europe.

One clue to the continental homeland of the Jutes is supplied by a comparison of the pottery and jewellery found in Kentish graves with similar objects found elsewhere in Europe. Some of the pottery, probably dating from the fifth century, is markedly similar to pottery found in Jutland and in Frisia, especially on the west coast of Jutland which provided, as it still provides, the most

14 *Silver brooch from Westbere*

28

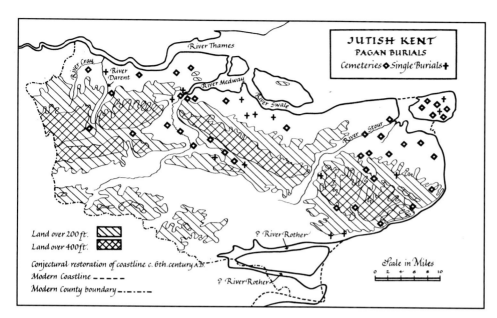

15 *Map showing pagan burials in Jutish Kent*

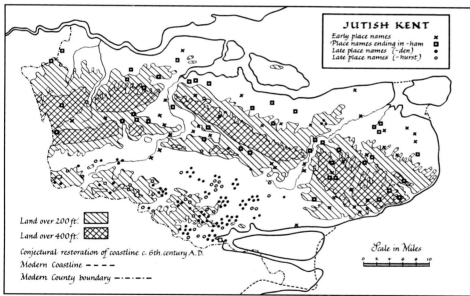

16 *The development of place names in Jutish Kent*

convenient point of embarkation for either England or Frisia. This seems to bear out the theory, precariously based on Bede's *History*, that the Jutes came from Jutland. On the other hand some pottery and jewellery found in Kent resembles pottery and jewellery from the land of the middle Rhine, a district which in the fifth century was predominantly Frankish. Moreover, there were some similarities between the legal codes of the Kentish kings and certain Frankish codes and there are a number of place-name resemblances between

Kent and the middle Rhine district. One possible interpretation of this evidence is that the first migrants (to call them invaders is scarcely polite if they were really responding to an invitation from Vortigern) came from Jutland and Frisia, and that later there was a separate Frankish incursion. Alternatively it may be that the Franks, making their way towards the mouth of the Rhine, encountered men from Jutland and Frisia who had also been caught up in the great folk-wandering and made common cause with them in trying their fortunes across the North Sea, finally settling together in Kent. The term 'Jutes' seems not to have come into use for a couple of centuries after the time of Hengist. To themselves these people were the 'Kentings', that is the men living in Kent. The fact that they had no racial name for themselves, as the Angles and Saxons had, suggests strongly that the Kentings were not a single race, all originating from a common homeland on the Continent.

The exact manner of the Jutish conquest of Kent we do not know. That it was different in character from the Roman invasion or the Norman Conquest is certain. The Jutes came, families and all, with the intention of settling here, because, for reasons which today are only partly understood, they felt driven to leave their European homelands. In the earliest phases, when there was fighting to be done, it must have been an organised expedition, but after the first settlements had been made stragglers continued to cross the North Sea for many years, perhaps for two or three generations.

According to later tradition the Britons who inhabited Kent either fled to the west, and eventually to the mountain fastnesses of Wales, or were exterminated by the Jutes. These must have been the fates of some of them, but of how many we cannot judge. Some remained as the slaves of the conquerors—Walmer, for example, means the sea-coast of the *weallas*, or slaves. The fact that few British place-names survive seems at first sight to support the tradition that the Britons either fled or were exterminated, but in some other parts of the country, where British survival is known from archaeological evidence, British place-names are scanty. In Saxon times the population of Kent was probably well under 50,000, so there must have been ample room for two races to dwell in the region without coming into perpetual conflict, especially if, as seems not unlikely, the Britons for the most part kept to the hills, and the Jutes to the valleys. But this is conjecture, and the truth is that we really know little about the relations between Jutes and Britons.

The Anglo-Saxon Chronicle (which began to be compiled in the reign of King Alfred as a year-by-year account of events of importance and is not therefore a first-hand and reliable record of affairs which happened two or three hundred years earlier) says that Æsc (or Oisc), who claimed to be a direct descendant of Hengist, reigned as king of Kent from 488 until 512. The kingdom of Kent had probably much the same boundaries as the modern county, and small though it was compared with the other English kingdoms, King Æthelberht, a great-grandson of Æsc who reigned in Kent from 560 to 616, was Bretwalda, or overlord, of all the provinces south of the Humber. In the latter part of the seventh century the throne of Kent seems to have been held by intruders from Wessex, but from 695 to 725 Kent was reigned over by

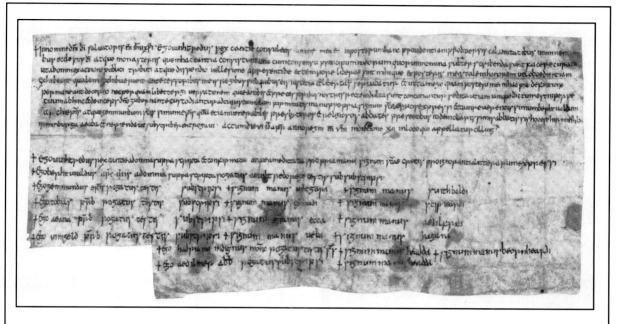

Translation

† In the name of the Lord God our saviour, Jesus Christ, I, Wihtred, King of Kent, having regard for the future of my soul, have taken care to make this provision because of diverse misfortunes threatening the churches of God and the monasteries which exist in this [Kingdom of] Kent, with the consent of my chief men whose names are to be written below; that athey may be free from all public tax, tribute, charge or vexation from the present day and time; and they show to me and those who come after me such honour and obedience as they have shown to my royal ancestors under whom justice and liberty wre secured for them; and I decree that both I and those who come after me shall persevere in this pious determination, nor by any subterfuge whatever are those things to be impaired which by us and our predecessors have been rightly granted, but as is now declared at this time they are henceforth continuously and for ever to be preserved, with the Lord's guidance; in full confirmation of this I have with my own hand represented the sign of the Holy Cross and I have requested the most reverend Berhtwald, the archbishop, and the most holy bishop Gemmund, to subscribe, as well as venerable priests and the religious abbots, there being present the most renowned abbesses, that is Hirminhilda, Irminburga, Aeaba and Nerienda. Done, the sixth day of the Ides of April in the eighth year of our reign, in the twelfth indiction, at the place which is called Cilling. [Cilling has not been certainly identified.]

† I, Wihtred, King of Kent, being ignorant of letters, to all that is above-written and confirmed and dictated by me have with my own hand represented the sign of the Holy Cross.

[The chief men whose names follow are Berhtwald, archbishop, Gemmund, bishop, Tobias, priest, Aeana, priest, Uinigeld, Cyniad, Ecca, Ueba, Hadrian, monk, Aedilmer, abbot, Suithbald, Scirieard, Aedilfrid, Hagana, Headda, Headda, Beornheard.]

17 *The Charter of King Wihtred, A.D. 699*

its lawful sovereign, King Wihtred. He was noted for his zeal and piety; in the County Archives Office at Maidstone can be seen the charter whereby in 699 he granted the churches and monasteries in Kent freedom from taxation.

Wihtred was succeeded by his son Eadbert, and he in turn was followed by his brother, another Æthelberht, whose death in 760 brought to an end the Kentish royal line that traced its descent back through a period of three hundred years to Æsc. Soon afterwards Kent came under the overlordship of Mercia. The Battle of Otford in 774 was a rising of the Kentish men against Offa, their Mercian overlord, and it is likely that as a result of the battle Kent regained its independence for a few more years. In 805 it became once more a province of Mercia, a status which it retained for only 20 years, for in 825 Egbert of Wessex defeated Beornwulf of Mercia in a decisive battle near Swindon, and Kent, submitting to Egbert, ceased to be a separate kingdom.

Of the kings of Kent the most famous is certainly the first Æthelberht, who held the throne from 560 to 616. It was in his day that St Augustine, landing near Ebbsfleet, made his way to the king's court at Canterbury, bringing with him the Christian gospel. The Christian religion was no novelty to Æthelberht for his wife Bertha, the daughter of the Frankish king Charibert whose capital was at Paris, was herself a Christian and she continued to practise her own religion at her husband's court. Æthelberht met Augustine in Thanet, according to tradition in the open air for the king was fearful of the magic that the missionary might be bringing with him (Æthelberht seems to have learnt little from his wife about her religion; was Christianity then thought of, perhaps, as

18 *Otford, scene of vital battles*

I *Richborough Castle. In the foreground is the third-century Roman fort, in the middle distance the late third-century Roman walls, and through the gap is the mid-20th-century electrical engineering plant.*

II *Lullingstone Roman villa. This part of the mosaic floor depicts Jupiter, in the form of a white bull, abducting Europa while accompanied by two cupids. This floor is dated to about the middle of the fourth century.*

III *Part of historic Maidstone, showing the river Medway and a group of medieval buildings. On the left is the Archbishop's Palace, in the centre is All Saints Church, and on the extreme right the remains of the old medieval college.*

IV *Aylesford's historic bridge at low water. The small centre arches were converted into the single large arch shown here some years ago to permit navigation up the Medway to Maidstone.*

a religion for women rather than for men?) Augustine was allowed to preach, and to use St Martin's church at Canterbury, a church which had been founded during the Roman occupation and had probably served as the chapel of Queen Bertha. Soon Æthelberht himself and many of his people underwent conversion. Augustine began to build new churches and to restore some of those dating from the time of the Roman occupation; that they still stood and had not been destroyed during the Jutish invasion argues against the view that that had been an operation accompanied by wholesale violence and devastation.

Towards the end of 597 Augustine was consecrated bishop. On Christmas Day, 597, he reported, no fewer than 10,000 people were baptised—an astonishingly large number considering the then population of the kingdom; but perhaps in his report the bishop allowed enthusiasm to outrun statistical accuracy. Seven years later a second Kentish bishopric was established, at Rochester, with Justus as the first bishop. Bishoprics were created at London and elsewhere, but no other English kingdom at this period had two bishoprics. Kent was thus favoured probably because it was an unusually populous kingdom, with an unusually large proportion of Christians. Of Justus's cathedral church we know a little. It stood slightly to the west of the present cathedral, the west porch of which covers the eastern apsidal end of the earliest building. It was quite small, about 60 ft. long by 30 ft. wide. At Canterbury the oldest church buildings are St Martin's, which has already been referred to, the Abbey of St Augustine, and St Pancras', a little late sixth- or early-seventh century chapel within the Abbey curtilage.

19 *St Martin's church*

Augustine died within a few years of coming to Kent, and was succeeded as bishop of Canterbury by Laurentius. Elsewhere the new religion made little progress. Æthelberht persuaded Rædwald, king of the East Saxons, to adopt Christianity, but his successors drove Bishop Mellitus from London, and in his flight to Gaul Mellitus was joined by Bishop Justus of Rochester. This sudden worsening of the position of Christians in Kent followed the death of Æthelberht in 616, and the succession of his son Eadbald, who still clung to the heathen religion. Laurentius bravely stayed on at Canterbury, persuaded Eadbald to accept baptism, and within a few years Christianity in Kent, though not in other parts of England, was once more flourishing under royal protection. There was never again a danger of Kent reverting to heathenism, but it was many years before the whole of England had been converted to the new faith; the neighbouring Sussex, for example, cut off as it was from contact with Kent by the almost inpenetrable Wealden forest, remained heathen until Bishop Wilfrid, exiled from Northumbria in 680, spent some years among the South Saxons converting them to the faith which the men of Kent had professed for three generations.

Augustine not merely brought back the Christian religion to Canterbury, to Kent and to England, he also restored the contacts with the civilisation of Southern Europe which had lapsed early in the fifth century. Kent once again was on the highway from Rome to London. In 668 the learned Theodore was sent from Rome to be archbishop at Canterbury, and he was accompanied by a man no less learned than himself, Hadrian, who became Abbot of the monastery of SS Peter and Paul (the earlier dedication of St Augustine's) at Canterbury. Theodore brought order and organisation into the life of the English Church, and it was probably in his time that the development of the parochial system began. Under his influence and that of Hadrian, Canterbury became a centre of learning, of brilliant intellectual life, which attracted scholars from afar. The reputation which the Venerable Bede gave Canterbury for classical learning makes it appear to be without rival in that field throughout northern and western Europe.

It was partly under ecclesiastical influence, partly following the practice of the Franks, that the Kentish kings began to enact series of laws. To make a law seems to us a normal act of government; to the more primitive mind it is so abnormal as to be almost impossible. Laws were thought of as being divinely inspired, and for men to attempt to alter them would be the height of impiety— it is impossible, for example, to imagine Moses tampering with the laws which he had received on Mount Sinai. The first Kentish king to issue a set of laws was Æthelberht. The date of their issue must be later than 597 when Augustine came to Canterbury, but earlier than 616 when Æthelberht died. Another series was issued by Kings Hlothhere and Eadric in 685, and a third by King Wihtred in 695.

No attempt was made in these series of laws to set out the whole of the law in the form of a code. It was only the new laws, or alterations to the old, which were published in this way. To publish the ordinary law was regarded as unnecessary, because it was already known to everyone. For this reason it is not, alas! known to us.

The legislation of the Kentish kings of the seventh century included laws protecting the Church and exempting it from taxation; forbidding heathen practices; laying down the manner in which lawsuits were to be determined; and instituting an elaborate system of money compensations for personal injuries—6s. for a broken arm, 12s. for an ear struck off, 50s. for an eye, 1s. for a back tooth, and so on. This may sound barbarous, but it is really more civilised than the *lex talionis*, an eye for an eye and a tooth for a tooth, and probably the new law reflected the influence of the Church.

The laws of Æthelberht have a special interest in that they are the earliest extant document written in the English language. Kent's position in the van of the new learning and civilisation is demonstrated by the fact that the oldest Wessex code of laws dates only from about A.D.690—nearly a century later than the laws of Æthelberht.

This account of the Kentish royal house, of the Church, with Canterbury at its centre, and of the issue of legal codes may suggest a greater degree of organisation, stability and uniformity than Kent at that time enjoyed. The Jutish settlement and colonisation of Kent was a long-drawn out process, and parts of the county, indeed, remained unoccupied until shortly before the Norman Conquest. From archaeological discoveries, and from place-names, it is possible to determine in which parts of Kent settlement first took place and which parts were the last to be colonised. Cemeteries in which, along with the dead, are buried objects for their use in a future life, belong to the heathen period. Such

21 *Brooch from Cuxton ('Ælfgivu owns me')*

22 *Penny of the Archbishop Ceolnoth, mid-ninth century*

cemeteries have been found at many places—e.g. Sarre, Patrixbourne, Crundale, Kingston, Faversham, Milton Regis, Northfleet, Horton Kirby and since then at Lyminge and Broadstairs. Many of the graves have yielded specimens of Kentish jewellery (examples can be seen at Maidstone Museum and elsewhere) of such magnificence as to testify to the wealth at least of the upper classes. These pagan cemeteries are shown on the map on page 29, and indicate settlements that must have been established by about the end of the sixth century.

Shown on the next map are certain place-names which are known to be of an early type. These include heathen names like Woodnesborough, *Woden's Hill*, and Wye, the place of the idols; names originally ending in *-ingas*, which meant a group of people—Hawkinge, e.g. was the people of *Hawk*, Malling the people of *Mealla*; names like Eastry, Sturry, Lyminge; and names whose original termination was *ham*, a homestead or settlement.

As the maps show, the archaeological and the place-name evidence largely coincide in indicating those parts of the county which were the earliest to be settled by the Jutes. They were the valleys of the Lesser Stour, the Great Stour, the Medway and the Darent; Thanet (though the paucity of early place-names here is surprising); the fertile country on either side of the line of Watling Street; and the foot of the Downs in East Kent. These areas were the first to be occupied, partly because they were easy of access, but still more because of the favourable conditions that they offered—a kindly soil, availability of water, and little to be done in the way of tree-clearing. It was otherwise in the Weald and on the dip slope of the North Downs, where not only did the soil consist of heavy clay that was hard to work, but also the whole area was covered with dense forest. In time it was found that the Wealden forest had its value, for it could be used for feeding swine and many of the upland villages had their swine-pastures, or 'dens', in the Weald. *Den* and *ley* are still common terminations of place-names in the Weald; probably these offshoots of earlier upland settlements, some of which are shown on the map on page 29, came into existence in the eighth or ninth century, although some are as late as the eleventh.

One other part of the county that was unattractive to the early settlers was the north-west with its hungry, sandy soil, marked today by the Commons of Bromley, Hayes, Keston and Chislehurst. It was natural that such 'less eligible' sites should be shunned by the first comers who had plenty of more desirable places to choose from.

The gradual colonisation of Kent did not proceed in peace. As, in the fifth century the Jutes crossed the sea to invade south-eastern Britain, so now they were followed in the ninth century by the Danes. The story of the Danish raids can be reconstructed from the entries in the Anglo-Saxon Chronicle. They first appear in 832, when 'heathen men overran the Isle of Sheppey'. Nine years later Rochester and Canterbury suffered severely at their hands, and in 851 the Danes for the first time made their winter-quarters in England, in the Isle of Thanet. Three years later they wintered in Sheppey. In 865 they broke a treaty of peace made with the men of Kent, and overran the eastern part of the county. Twenty years later Rochester was besieged, but Alfred was now on the throne and the defences of England were being taken in hand. He relieved the town, the Danes departed, and the newly-formed English fleet defeated a small Danish fleet at Stourmouth (which at this time stood on the arm of the sea which separated Thanet from the mainland). The most serious threat of all was the incursion of 893. One Danish army, which had been harrying France, crossed the Channel from Boulogne and with 250 ships entered the mouth of the Limen, or Rother, which then probably flowed out into the sea near Hythe. They towed their ships four miles up river and built a fort at Appledore. Meanwhile another Danish army under Hasten with 80 ships sailed into the Thames estuary and constructed a fort on the Swale marshes near Milton Regis. Earthworks which may be the sites of these forts still exist. From these two camps in the following year the Danes broke out and plundered southern England, from time to time clashing with the armies of King Alfred; but this campaign belongs to the general history of England, not to the particular history of Kent. Throughout the 10th century there was intermittent raiding in Kent, but the Danes never were able to make any permanent lodgment here, as they did in the midlands and the north, and Kent never came under Danish influence, much less under Danish domination. This accounts for the complete absence of Danish place-names in Kent.

In their earlier raids the Danes were prompted by hopes of plunder, not of permanent settlement. The towns, such as Rochester and Canterbury, were prosperous, the monasteries were wealthy, and towns and monasteries both held out good prospect of booty. The oldest of the Kent monastic houses, those

23 *The 'Saxon Oval' at Dover Castle*

at Canterbury and Rochester, were founded by King Æthelberht at the time of Augustine's mission, and several others, including those at Dover, Folkestone, Lyminge, Reculver, Minster-in-Sheppey and Minster-in-Thanet, were established before the end of the seventh century. Their position, incidentally, is additional evidence as to the parts of the county which were the first to be settled and developed by the Jutes. It was these same areas which attracted the unwelcome attention of the Danes, and all of the monasteries suffered severely. Several of them ceased to exist, the buildings being utterly destroyed (although the nunnery at Folkestone may have been ruined by the encroachment of the sea rather than by the Danes), and they remained in abeyance until their revival in the more law-abiding years of the 11th century.

In spite of the raids of the 'heathen men' from across the North Sea, learning survived in the monasteries. At Canterbury, in particular, illuminated manuscripts were being produced in the 10th and 11th centuries which show a vivid mastery of the art of line-drawing. Late Saxon sculpture also achieved an astonishingly high standard, although Kent unfortunately possesses little of it, the cross from Reculver being almost the only example. Few buildings of Saxon date have survived. This is understandable enough, for even the houses of the great, and important buildings like churches, were constructed very generally of timber,

24 *The ruins of St Mary, Reculver*

whilst the poor lived in hovels the life of which cannot have been much longer than that of a modern hen-run. Where churches were built of stone, as at Canterbury Cathedral, St Augustine's Abbey and Rochester Cathedral, the early structures were afterwards demolished to make way for larger buildings. Several parish churches, including St Mary in Dover Castle, Lyminge, Cheriton, Lydd, Paddlesworth (near Folkestone) and Whitfield, contain more or less extensive remnants of Saxon work. But Kent has nothing to compare with, for example, the Saxon church of Earl's Barton in Northamptonshire.

Saxon Kent of the 11th century, like the rest of England, was mainly a land of country-dwellers, although Canterbury, Rochester, Dover, Sandwich, Hythe, Romney and Fordwich were reckoned as boroughs and were market and trading towns of some significance. Generally they were not closely built-up like the centre of a modern town, but at Canterbury the houses must have been close together because the customary law of the place required a space of at least two feet to be left between adjacent houses to serve as an 'eaves-drip'. Of industry as we know it there was none, although there were saltpans in several parts of the county and water-mills wherever streams existed to drive them. The majority of the people lived, directly or indirectly, by agriculture.

The farming tool which was distinctive of Kent was the turn-wrest plough. It could plough along one furrow and down the next, whereas with the midland plough it was necessary to plough in furlongs. This gave the Kentish fields a different appearance and perhaps a different shape from those in other parts of the country, and to some extent these differences are still observable. But for the ordinary farm-worker one part of England must have been very much like another, and Ælfric's *Colloquies* (written about the year 1000) tells us with vivid directness the kind of life which ordinary people lived in the Middle Ages. For many centuries this was their manner of life, after as well as before the Norman Conquest. The immediate effects of the Conquest can easily be exaggerated. The Normans undoubtedly imported an element of efficiency into English life, particularly in the building of castles, the building of churches and in the organisation of secular and ecclesiastical government. But it would be wrong to think of pre-Conquest Kent or pre-Conquest England as being a backward and barbaric province, to be awakened from its sloth only by the civilising embrace of Normandy.

4

The Norman Conquest and Settlement

25 *Normans crossing the Channel*

The landing of Duke William in 1066 was by no means the first contact between England and Normandy. King Edward the Confessor was in close communication with Normandy, and an affray in 1051 between the retinue of his guest and brother-in-law, Count Eustace of Boulogne, and the men of Dover was a foretaste of what was to happen 15 years later. The various accounts of the squabble at Dover are conflicting, but the outlines are clear. Eustace was either on his way to or from the court of Edward in London, and naturally his route lay by way of the port of Dover. There Eustace's men began demanding quarters, evidently in a high-handed fashion. High words soon gave place to blows, a Norman was killed and thereupon Eustace in revenge slew 20 townsmen. The men of Dover rose and drove out the Normans, killing several of them. With the survivors of his retinue Eustace escaped to London and complained to the King of the treatment which he had suffered at Dover. Edward resolved that the town should be punished, and ordered Earl Godwin to deal faithfully with the town according to its deserts.

Such an order placed Godwin in a quandary. He was closely connected with Kent; he was Earl of all the shires of southern England, including this county; the offce of earl, although a royal appointment, had become almost hereditary, and Godwin's family was the most powerful in the kingdom, with the throne itself not beyond their grasp; and Godwin had reason to believe that Eustace's men were at least as much to blame as the townsmen for the affray at Dover. He was reluctant to punish his own town and people of Dover, but to disobey the royal command was near to rebellion. He decided to take the risk, assembled an army at Tetbury in Gloucestershire and delivered what looks like a discreet ultimatum to the King. The King also assembled an army, and although a clash was prevented by a desire on both sides for compromise, the compromise was a moral defeat for Godwin who went into exile on the Continent, his son Harold seeking safety in Ireland.

The departure of his over-mighty subjects Godwin and Harold gave Edward the opportunity of strengthening the Norman element at his court, and in 1051 or 1052 he received a visit from Duke William himself. But Godwin was not the man to submit to permanent exile, and in 1052 he returned, landing at Dungeness. He received promises of support from men in Kent, Sussex and Surrey, and after securing similar promises from a number of south coast ports

40

and towns (promises sometimes extorted under duress) he made contact with his son Harold, returning from exile in Ireland. Collecting together a fleet from Pevensey, Romney, Hythe and Folkestone, Godwin and Harold enticed to them the seamen of Kent and Sussex. The King's fleet lay at Sandwich, but its attempts to intercept Godwin were ineffective, and it withdrew to London. At Dover and at Sandwich Godwin landed and took ships and hostages, before following the King's fleet up the Thames towards London. On his way he found time to plunder the Isle of Sheppey and to burn the town of Milton Regis (for it was a royal vill). At London the King's fleet was surrounded by the more numerous ships of Godwin, but hostilities were avoided, Godwin and Harold were received back into the King's 'full friendship', Edward sent away his French advisers, and Bishop Stigand, bishop of Winchester, was appointed to the archbishopric of Canterbury, which the Norman Robert was arbitrarily declared to have vacated. Norman influence in England was at the lowest ebb which it reached during Edward's reign.

The events of the remainder of his reign do not particularly concern Kent. He died on 5 January 1066, and was succeeded by Godwin's son Harold, but as the author of the Chronicle wrote, 'He enjoyed little tranquillity therein the while that he wielded the kingdom'. In May Harold's brother Tostig, crossing from beyond the sea, harried the south coast and occupied Sandwich. Harold suspected that Tostig was acting in concert with Duke William, and that the Normans would speedily make use of the bridgehead which Tostig had secured. Harold therefore collected a large force, naval and military to recover Sandwich, but Tostig, when he heard of the King's preparations, departed northwards, taking some of the portsmen, willing or unwilling, with him; he eventually joined forces with Harold Hardrada, king of Norway, when in the late summer he invaded the north-east coast of England.

It was whilst Harold of England was engaged in defending his kingdom against Harold of Norway that William of Normandy landed at Pevensey in Sussex. After a few days he removed unmolested to a more secure position at Hastings, and there constructed a wooden castle. A number of ships bringing up reinforcements, through faulty information or faulty navigation, made for Romney where they were fiercely attacked by the portsmen who soon paid for their boldness. Five days after the Battle of Hastings William began to advance towards London, but recognising the strategic importance of Kent, and the necessity of securing his line of communication with Normandy, he did not advance directly north-westward through the Weald (the nature of the country would in any case have discouraged such an enterprise), but turned eastward along the coast into Kent. Romney was severely punished for having dared to resist the Normans a few days before. Dover was William's next objective, and it surrendered on demand. He stayed there eight days, building works of fortification, and then he moved on to Canterbury, where he remained for a month. It was a cautious advance, for William was feeling his way as he went. Whilst he was at Canterbury he negotiated with other important places in southern England about their submission. Eventually he felt secure enough to

26 *Duke William of Normandy*

27 *Normans burning a house, probably at Dover*

resume his advance towards London, which accepted him although not until after the Normans had displayed their military strength in a great encircling movement which took them as far to the west as Wallingford in Berkshire.

A story is told of William's march from Canterbury to London which deserves to be repeated because, although it is well known, and well known to be fictitious, it can be regarded as possessing symbolic truth. Whilst William was advancing westward from Rochester, over the hill at Swanscombe, he saw himself gradually surrounded by what appeared to be a moving forest. Suddenly the forest resolved itself into an army of archers, camouflaged like Macduff's army on its march from Birnam to Dunsinane with green boughs of trees (although it was the month of November!). At their head stood Stigand, Archbishop of Canterbury, and Egelnoth, Abbot of St Augustine's, who demanded for the men of Kent confirmation of their ancient laws and immunities. Recovering from his astonishment and fear, William was glad to grant their request.

Thus the story runs. The truth is more probably that, as he advanced from Dover to Canterbury, William received the submission of the men of Kent, and promised recognition of their ancient liberties and customs. This supposition is in part borne out by the account given by the Conqueror's chaplain, William of Poitiers, who wrote that the 'men of Kent of their own accord met [Duke William] not far from Dover, swore allegiance and gave hostages'. A promise to recognise the customs of Kent would be quite in keeping with the character of the Conquest, as it was envisaged by William at that time. He was anxious to assert the legality of his succession and the continuity of government; he came not as an innovator but as one who stood for tradition and he established order (*conquer* was later said to be a technical legal term for obtaining possession of property to which a man had a lawful claim and William was *conqueror*, therefore, in two senses). During the first three or four years after the Battle of Hastings his policy was to govern through the great English families and to win over their support, rather than to supplant them by his Norman followers. There is therefore nothing surprising in his allowing the men of Kent to retain their old customs and laws, especially as they were of a kind which would not be likely to embarrass the king's government, being mainly concerned with land-tenure.

The most distinctive of the laws or customs of Kent was Gavelkind. This was the name given to the tenure wherby most of the land in Kent was then held. Its important features were these: on a man's death his land was divided between all his sons equally instead of going wholly to the eldest; a widow was entitled to dower in one-half of her late husband's land, instead of one-third as elsewhere in England; a man whose wife had died was entitled to one-half of her land for life, whereas in the rest of the country he took the whole for life, provided that a child had been born of the marriage; and although elsewhere if a man was found guilty of felony his lands were forfeit to the Crown, in Kent his heirs immediately succeeded to his estate.

In 1067 William returned temporarily to Normandy, leaving as regents during his absence William FitzOsbern, his seneschal, and Odo, bishop of Bayeux, William's half-brother, to whom he had confided the earldom of Kent. That

William should have entrusted Kent to a powerful magnate like Odo shows that he was fully conscious of its importance as the link between his kingdom of England and his duchy of Normandy. Odo established himself at Dover Castle (a wooden-fortification that preceded the existing great stone keep), but whilst he was away dealing with a rebellion north of the Thames there was a rising in Kent and the insurgents sent an invitation to Count Eustace of Boulogne, who had quarrelled with William, to land at Dover which, he was promised, would readily submit. Eustace crossed the Channel and on landing was joined by a large number of English, but their attempt on the castle failed, and Eustace quickly withdrew to Boulogne before Odo could return to Dover. William was faced with unrest in other parts of the country, and in 1069 a Danish fleet appeared off the Kent coast. Landings were attempted at Dover and Sandwich but were driven off, and the fleet sailed away to the north, eventually finding an anchorage in the River Humber.

If William's original policy was to confirm the English magnates in their possessions and to govern through them, the risings and unrest during the first four or five years after the Conquest made him reverse this policy and strengthen the position of his Norman followers. He allotted to them the lands not only of the English who had fallen at the Battle of Hastings, but also of those who had failed to make their submission or who had joined in the risings which troubled the north and west. In Kent much of the land was held by the Church, and no attempt was made to disturb it in its possessions. So far was William prepared to go to avoid trouble that he even allowed Stigand to remain as archbishop of Canterbury, in spite of the facts that he had been thrust into the office to replace the Norman Robert, that Robert had never vacated the see, and that Stigand continued to hold the bishopric of Winchester in plurality with the archbishopric.

In April 1070, the Pope sent a mission to England to straighten out the affairs of the Church. It is unlikely that William actually asked for the mission, but undoubtedly he approved of it. One of its first acts was to remove Stigand from the offices which he held. To succeed him as archbishop, William secured Lanfranc, an Italian by birth, who was abbot of the of the monastery of St Stephen at Caen in Normandy, and a scholar with a European reputation. He had been one of the Duke's oldest and most intimate advisers and his appointment as archbishop strengthened William's position. Common to them both was a respect for order and organisation, which Lanfranc introduced into the affairs of the Church as William did into the secular government of the country. Hitherto secular and ecclesiastical government had been confused; William ordained that they should be kept separate and that in the shire court the bishop should no longer sit with the earl on the bench. Secular cases were to be dealt with by the earl in the shire court, and spiritual matters by the bishop in his court.

That William had no objection, in principle, to an English bishop is shown by the fact that Siward of Rochester, who gave no trouble and seems to have been of inconspicuous character, was allowed to retain his see.

A striking example of the organisation which William introduced into government was the compilation of Domesday Book. After consulting his

TERRA HAMONIS VICECOMITIS
IN LEST DE WIWARLET. IN WIT HUND.
Hamo uicecom ten de rege un manerium.
qd T.R.E. se defd p. ii. solins 7 dimid. 7 m p uno
solin 7 iii. iugis. Tra. e. viii. car. In dnio. v. bou arantes.
7 xvi. uitti cu. xv. bord hnt. x. car. Ibi aecclā. 7 vii. serui.
7 un molin de. ix. solid. 7 lx. anguitt. Ibi. xx. ac pti.
7 silua. xxx. porc. 6. vi. den.
T.R.E. ualeb. x. lib. 7 post: vii. lib. Modo: xiiii. lib. 7 vi. solid.
De isto an ten Hugo de montfort. iii. iuga 7 dim. Val. lx. sol.
IN DIMIDIO LEST DE SUDTONE. IN GRENVIZ HUND.
Ibi ht haimo. lx iii. acs tre. que pan in holviz.
Wills acaptari tenuit de rege. E. Ibi sunt. xi. bord
reddtes xl i. denar. Totu ual. iii. lib.
IN LEST DE ELESFORD. IN LITEFEL HUND.
Ipse haimo ten MAROURDE. Norman tenuit de rege. E.
7 tc 7 m p. ii. solins se defd. Tra. e. ix. car. In dnio sunt. ii.
7 xx viii. uitti cu. xv. bord hnt. x. car. Ibi aecclā. 7 x.
serui. 7 ii. molini de. x. solid. 7 ii. piscar. de. ii. solid.
Ibi. xx. ac pti. 7 tant siluae unde exeunt. lx. porc de pasnag.
T.R.E. ualeb. xii. lib. 7 post: x. lib. Modo: xix. lib.
IN LEST DE BOROWART. IN WITESTAPLE HUND.
Ipse haimo ten BLEHEM. Norman tenuit de rege. E.
7 tc 7 m se defd p uno solin. Tra. e. iiii. car. 7 xii. uitti
hnt ibi. ii. car. In dnio. e una car. Ibi aecclā. 7 ii. ac pti.
7 de pasnag. lx. porc. Ibi una piscaria.
T.R.E. ualeb. viii. lib. 7 post 7 modo: ual. vi. lib.

28 *Part of a page of Domesday Book*

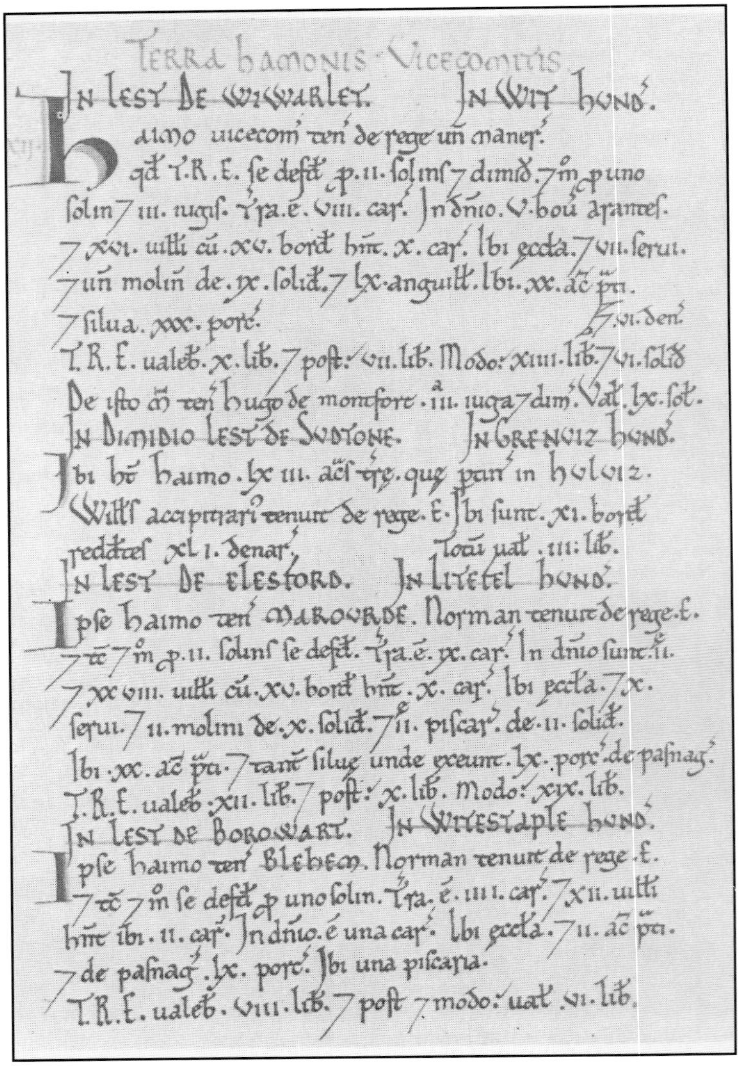

Translation

THE LAND OF HAMO THE SHERIFF

In the Lathe of Wye
In Wye Hundred
Hamo the Sheriff holds a manor from the King which answered for 2½ sulungs before 1066; now for 1 sulung and 3 yokes. Land for 8 ploughs. In lordship 5 ploughing oxen.
16 villigers with 15 smallholders have 10 ploughs.
A church; 7 slaves; a mill worth 9 s. and 60 eels.
Meadow 20 acres; woodland, 30 pigs.
Value before 1066 £10; later £7; now £14 6s. 6d.
Hugh de Montfort holds 3½ yokes of this manor.
Value 60s.

In the Half Lathe of Sutton.
In Greenwhich Hundred.
Hamo has 63 acres of land which belong to Woolwich. William the Falconer held them from King Edward.
11 smallholders who pay 41d.
Value of the whole £3.

In the Lathe of Aylesford.
In Littlefield Hundred
Hamo holds MEREWORTH himself. Norman held it from King Edward. Then and now it answered for 2 sulungs. Land for 9 ploughs. In lordship two.
28 villagers with 15 smallholders have 10 ploughs.
A church; 10 slaves; 2 mills at 10 s.; 2 fisheries at 2 s.
Meadow, 20 acres; as much woodland as produces 60 pigs in pasturage.
Value before 1066 £12; later £10; now £19.

In the Lathe of Borough.
In Whitstable Hundred
Hamo holds BLEAN himself. Norman held it from King Edward. Then and now it answered for 1 sulung. Land for 4 ploughs.
12 villagers have 2 ploughs.
In lordship 1 plough.
A church; meadow, 2 acres; from pasturage, 60 pigs; a fishery.
Value before 1066 £8; value later and now £6.

Council at Christmas, 1085, the King determined that an inquiry should be made into the ownership of every property throughout the length and breadth of the country—who had owned it in the time of King Edward the Confessor, how large it was, what its value was now, what had been its value formerly, how many men—villeins, cottagers, slaves, free men, etc.—were upon each estate, and how many cattle and swine. Within a year the vast inquiry had been completed and the returns sent in to the King. To collect the information commissioners were dispatched into each county, and to them came men from every locality who informed the commissioners, upon oath, about the ownership of land in their neighbourhood. From the way in which the Kent portion of Domesday Book is arranged it looks as though the commissioners began in

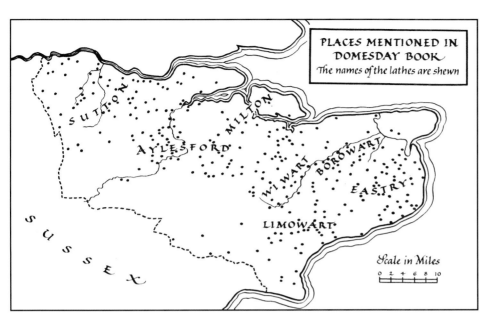

the western part of the county, moving eastward until they came to Canterbury and Dover.

About the great landowners of Kent we shall have more to say in the next chapter. Domesday Book tells us a good deal more about the county in the year 1086 than merely the names of the landowners. It begins with an account of Dover, which, it records, was burnt down just after King William came into England. This is doubtless a reference to the occupation of Dover by William on his way from Hastings to London. Another interesting item of information about the town is that a mill had recently been built near the entrance to the harbour (which lay inland from the present harbour) and so churned up the water that it endangered shipping.

Domesday Book then goes on to give the 'king's laws' (or rights) in Kent. At this period there was no Common Law, that is a law common to all parts of the kingdom; the law varied from place to place, and the Common Law was only gradually built up in the 12th and 13th centuries. Amongst the laws pertaining to Kent which Domesday Book records are these: if a man interferes with or commits a breach of the peace upon the public highway he must pay a heavy fine to the king; if the men of the county are summoned to a meeting of the shire court they are to go as far as Penenden Heath (near Maidstone; the ordinary meeting place of the court) but cannot be compelled to go farther; the king has a right to one-half of the forfeited goods of a thief condemned to death, the other half going to the man's own lord; if any man gives shelter to another who has been sentenced to exile a fine shall be paid to the king; except in the case of certain lands, which are named, the heirs of a man who dies shall pay to the king a 'relief', a kind of death-duty which became due before the heirs could succeed to the estate; and various owners of land owe the king special services, such as providing him with a bodyguard for six days at Canterbury or Sandwich.

After this recital of the 'king's laws' in Kent, Domesday Book records the other information which was collected by the commissioners in answer to their inquiries. The following (in translation) is typical of the entries which it contains:

In the Lathe of AYLESFORD
In LITTLEFIELD Hundred
Hamo holds MEREWORTH himself. Norman held it from King Edward. Then and now it answered for 2 sulungs. Land for 9 ploughs. In lordship 2.
28 villagers with 15 smallholders have 10 ploughs. A church; 10 slaves; 2 mills at 10s; 2 fisheries at 2s. Meadow, 20 acres; as much woodland as produces 60 pigs in pasturage.
Value before 1066 £12; later £10; now £19.

The general meaning of an entry like this is clear. In the year 1086 Hamo, the sheriff of Kent, held the estate of Mereworth from the king. The owner in King Edward's time had been a man named Norman. For purposes of taxation it was reckoned as two sulungs, a sulung being nominally about 160 acres. There was enough arable land to keep nine ploughs employed; on the land which Hamo himself farmed there were two ploughs, and on the land farmed by his tenants (*villeins* and *bordars*) there were 10 ploughs, making 12 in all, so there were rather more ploughs and plough-teams than the size of the holding really required. Like almost all towns and villages on a river or stream, Mereworth had a mill or two, probably quite small since the profits from them were estimated at only 10 shillings a year. The fisheries may have been of eels,

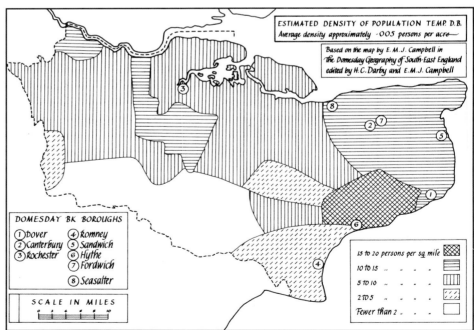

30 *Map showing the estimated population of Kent at the time of Domesday Book*

as they were in the adjacent parish of Yalding. At the time of King Edward the estate was considered to be worth £12 a year, but afterwards the value fell to £10, perhaps because in the uncertain years following immediately upon the Conquest the property was allowed to deteriorate. Evidently it had been improved by Hamo for its annual value by 1086 was regarded as £19.

Mereworth, in common with most villages in Kent, had a church at the time of Domesday Book, doubtless a wooden structure, of which no trace has survived. It also had a few slaves, or serfs. There was a later tradition that serfdom never existed in Kent, but Domesday Book shows that quite a considerable number of the inhabitants of the county were reckoned in this class; however, conditions were so far from being uniform that this does not necessarily mean that they had the same rights and duties as serfs in other parts of the country. The exact status of the various categories of men who are referred to—*villeins, bordars, cottagers, serfs, sokemen*—is a difficult and technical subject, which the most learned scholars have not yet explained to each others' satisfaction.

One other point to be noticed in the Mereworth entry is the reference to woodland which was used as swine pasture. The swine were fed on the acorns of the oak woodland of the Weald. The woodland belonging to Mereworth must have been extensive, as Mereworth Woods still are, for the rent for

31 *St Margaret's at Cliffe, considered by many to be the finest Norman parish church in the county*

32 *Swineherd in oak forest*

'pannage', that is the right to depasture swine in the woodland, was no less than 60 swine a year.

Information of this kind is given for the whole of Kent with the significant exception of the Weald (see the map on page 46). As already explained, this was the last part of the county to be colonised by the Saxons. Many of the upland towns and villages possessed the right to pasture their swine in certain areas of the Wealden forest. Thus, to give two examples: *Tenterden* means the swine-pasture belonging to the men of Thanet; and hundreds of years after the time of Domesday Book the manor of Chilham was one of those which had rights in the Weald—in this case in Frittenden, Headcorn, Smarden, Egerton and Goudhurst. The attachment of 'dens' in the Weald to upland properties resulted in their not being separately recorded in Domesday Book, and undoubtedly at this time the Weald was only thinly populated.

Salt-pans are referred to at several places near the Channel coast and the Thames estuary, e.g. at Milton Regis, Faversham, Oare, Ospringe, Graveney, Boughton-under-Blean, Reculver, Chislet (with no fewer than 47 salt-pans), Monkton, Minster-in-Thanet, Eastry, Folkestone, Romney Marsh, Eastbridge and Bilsington.

From Domesday Book it is possible to hazard a guess about the population of Kent in the reign of William the Conqueror. The total of the landowners; tenants, villeins, cottagers, burgesses and serfs mentioned under the various towns and villages amounts to between 12,000 and 13,000. This suggests that, including women and children, the population of the county was somewhere between 40,000 and 50,000. Compared with most other counties Kent was fairly thickly peopled, though less so than East Anglia. The total population of England at the time of Domesday Book is estimated to have been very approximately, 1¼ million, so that Kent represented about one-thirtieth of the total—curiously enough very much the same proportion that it represents today.

5

Feudal Kent

Domesday Book also gives particulars of the estates belonging to the dozen or so great landowners who between them held the major part of the county. The essence of the feudal system was that every man (except the king) held his land from an overlord in return for certain services, which might be, for example, to provide a knight, or to pay a rent, in money or in kind, or to work on his lord's land. Generally, where land was held by a church or religious house it was free of any service. The tenants who held directly from the king (who might have tenants holding from them, and their tenants have sub-tenants, and so on) were called tenants-in-chief. According to feudal theory no man (except the king) could 'own' land; he 'held' it. The feudal system was not a foreign

33 *Map showing manors held at the time of Domesday Book*

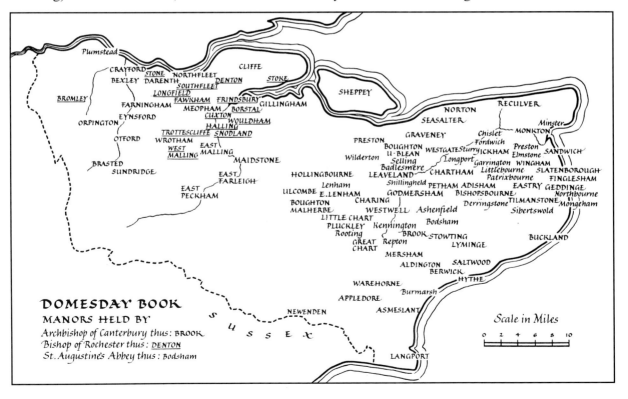

DOMESDAY BOOK
MANORS HELD BY
Archbishop of Canterbury thus: BROOK
Bishop of Rochester thus: DENTON
St. Augustine's Abbey thus: Bodsham

Scale in Miles

49

34 *The old courthouse, Milton Regis*

novelty introduced by the Normans; some of the rudiments of this method of land-holding can be traced in Saxon England. The Normans, with their efficient ways, made it more systematic, but the system began to crack and disintegrate almost as soon as the theory was fully worked out.

First amongst the great landowners in Kent was King William himself. He owned the enormous estate of Milton Regis, which was reckoned as no less than 84 sulungs and possessed extensive rights in the Weald; the smaller, but still important Faversham estate; and the two much smaller manors of Aylesford and Dartford.

The archbishop of Canterbury held the town of Sandwich, and about twenty-five manors scattered over the county. Among the larger were Otford, Wrotham, Maidstone and Charing, in each of which the remains of a medieval, though not Norman, farmhouse (usually called a 'palace') can still be seen. Larger manors which belonged to the archbishop were those of Wingham and Aldington. The monastery of Christ Church also held extensive estates. Monkton, a large manor of about 20 sulungs assessment, records in its name its former attachment to Christ Church. Adisham, another of the monastery's possessions, was almost as large as Monkton.

The bishop of Rochester's lands were on a much more modest scale. They all lay west of the Medway, save Borstal and Wouldham which are on the east bank of the river and most of them were within a dozen or fifteen miles of Rochester. The bishop held no lands within the diocese of Canterbury whereas the archbishop had several manors within the diocese of Rochester.

Vastly more powerful and wealthy than the bishop of Rochester was the bishop of Bayeux, Odo, upon whom William conferred the earldom of Kent. He was given nearly 200 Kentish manors, and he held something like 250 in other parts of the country. His Kentish estates were scattered over most of the county, the largest being those at Hoo (assessed at 33 sulungs and containing six churches) and at Folkestone (40 sulungs, with five churches). Other manors of considerable size held by Odo were those at Lessness, Swanscombe, Seal, Hadlow, Birling, Burham, Boxley, Chatham, Ospringe, Eastling, Patrixbourne, Barham and Elham.

35 *Rochester Castle*

But, extensively endowed with lands as he already was, Odo nonetheless contrived to get into his hands property to which he was not entitled. In 1076 Archbishop Lanfranc brought a lawsuit against him in the Shire Court at Penenden Heath for the recovery of the Church's purloined property. The trial lasted for three days. The court was presided over by Geoffrey, bishop of Coutances. All doubtful points were settled according to the practice which prevailed in England before the Conquest, and the elderly Æthelric, who had recently been deposed from the bishopric of Selsey, was brought to Penenden Heath in a cart in order to advise the court because he knew the Anglo-Saxon law. Here is another illustration that King William wanted to appear as the legitimate successor to Edward the Confessor, not as an innovator whose only claim to the throne lay in the power of the sword. The result of the Penenden Heath trial was that Lanfranc recovered 25 manors of which Odo had wrongly become possessed.

Early in his reign William conferred upon Battle Abbey the great manor of Wye which in Saxon times had been a royal possession. William had founded the abbey on the site of his battle, not so much in commemoration of his victory as in penance for the men whose deaths he had caused; for the Church set a penance upon men who committed homicide, notwithstanding that the death occurred in battle. The estate which William granted to his newly-established abbey was much more extensive than the modern village (or town) of Wye. It included rights over a large area of the Weald, and it also included Dengemarsh, with the right to wrecks and whales stranded on that part of the coast.

St Augustine's Abbey at Canterbury was another of the great landowning religious houses. It possessed some thirty manors, all but one of them (Plumstead) in east Kent. The largest were those at Minster-in-Thanet and Northbourne. The abbey's manor of Minster and the Christ Church estates at Monkton must, between them, have occupied a great part of the Isle of Thanet.

There is a revealing sentence in the Domesday Book entry about Minster to the effect that three knights hold, as tenants of the abbey, land which 'is worth nine pounds when there is peace in the country'. Thanet was a part of the realm where the peace had often been disturbed by the depredations of the Danes.

Another tenant-in-chief holding only one manor, that of Lewisham, was the Abbey of Ghent in Flanders. The manor had been given to the abbey by a daughter or niece of King Alfred who had married an earl of Flanders and thus it had already been in the Abbey's hands for nearly two hundred years. The grant had been confirmed by Edward the Confessor, another example of the contact which existed between his court and Flanders and Normandy.

The Canons of the Church of St Martin of Dover held a good many manors in east Kent which, although each was quite small, came to the very respectable total of 24 sulungs—probably something like 4,000 acres of arable land.

All the manors so far mentioned (except the four in the possession of the king himself) were held by men or houses of religion—for Odo was bishop of Bayeux as well as earl of Kent. Between them they accounted for much the greater part of the county (see the map on page 49 of the lands held by the archbishop, the bishop of Rochester and St Augustine's Abbey). The lay tenants-in-chief were only four in number: Hugh de Montfort, Count Eustace of Boulogne, Richard of Tonbridge and Hamo the Sheriff. The first three fought with William at Hastings; these Kentish manors were part of their reward, but only Hugh de Montfort held many lands in the county and his holdings were on nothing like the same scale as those of Odo, or of the archbishop or St Augustine's Abbey. For the most part his manors lay in south-east Kent with his castle at Saltwood as their centre. There can be little doubt that Hugh de Montfort, a military man, was established there to protect and defend this vulnerable and vitally important corner of the county.

36 *The   seal   of Saltwood*

Eustace of Boulogne held Westerham and Boughton Aluph. Richard of Tonbridge held Yalding and East Barming, but he also possessed (though this is not mentioned in Domesday Book) the 'Lowy' of Tonbridge, in some respects almost a miniature county in itself and, again like Hugh de Montfort's possessions, dependent upon a castle which commanded an important strategic position.

As tenant-in-chief Hamo held only four estates, but he held several more manors as sub-tenant of other tenants-in-chief. The last, and the least, of the tenants-in-chief was Albert the Chaplain, who held Newington-next-Sittingbourne.

Domesday Book also refers to a number of boroughs, of which Dover, Canterbury and Rochester were in a category by themselves being 'royal boroughs' and acknowledging no overlord but the king. Romney, Sandwich, Hythe and Fordwich were included in the lands of one of the great lordships but they also possessed certain privileges and duties which distinguished them from the remainder of the estates of which they formed part. The 'little borough' of Seasalter was in still another category and belonged to the archbishop of Canterbury's kitchen; presumably it was the cook's perquisite.

The men of Dover were granted exemption from certain tolls and other impositions in return for duties which they undertook on behalf of the king.

They were required to supply the king with 20 ships, each manned by 21 men, for 15 days in the year. Moreover, they had to ferry the king's messengers across the Strait at tariffs which seem modest—3d. for the passage of a horse in winter, 2d. in the summer; this was for a boat manned by a steersman and one other helper. We also learn that, at the time of Domesday Book, Dover had a Guildhall.

Canterbury, judged from its stated value, was a larger town than Dover. Since the time of Edward the Confessor a number of houses had been demolished to make room for the city defences (no doubt a ditch and rampart) and the castle. This was a wooden erection to the east of the site on which the castle of stone was afterwards built.

Rochester was a much smaller town. In the time of Edward the Confessor its value was reckoned as only 100 shillings, but by 1086 this had increased to twenty pounds.

Sandwich, according to the Saxon Chronicle, was given in 1031 by Canute to Christ Church; thus the Chronicle entry runs:

> As soon as he [Canute] came to England he gave to Christ's Church in Canterbury the haven of Sandwich, and all the rights that arise therefrom, on either side of the haven; so that when the tide is highest and fullest, and there be a ship floating as near the land as possible, and there be a man standing upon the ship with a taper-axe in his hand whithersoever the large taper-axe might be thrown out of the ship, throughout all that land the ministers of Christ's Church should enjoy their rights.

37 *Dover Castle*

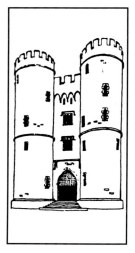

38 *Saltwood Castle gatehouse*

At the time of Domesday Book Sandwich belonged to the archbishop, paying an annual rent of fifty pounds and forty thousand herrings for the support of the monks of Christ Church. It rendered to the king the same sort of service (that is, in ships) as Dover rendered. Sandwich contained no fewer than 383 houses, so it was a sizeable town, probably as large as Canterbury.

Fordwich, a little borough with 73 houses, was also owned by the archbishop. Apparently in the time of King Edward it had owed ship-service as Dover and Sandwich did, but its service seems to have fallen into disuse by the reign of William the Conqueror. The information in Domesday Book about Hythe and Romney is less clear, because they were associated with other manors of the archbishop of Canterbury, but there is a reference to the sea-service which the men of Romney owed to the king. If the record were more complete we should probably find that the men of Hythe were under a similar obligation. Of that town it is recorded that 225 burgesses belonged to the manor of Saltwood, so the population of the borough is likely to have been in the neighbourhood of a thousand.

Domesday Book shows the way in which Kent was divided for administrative, judicial and taxation purposes into seven large divisions called lathes, or lests, and these in turn were sub-divided into smaller areas called hundreds. Lathes are peculiar to Kent; Sussex has its rapes, the northern counties their wapentakes, but Kent is the only county in which the major divisions are known as lathes. Their origin is certainly pre-Conquest and some historians believe that they date back to a quite early phase of the Jutish colonisation of Kent. Each was based on an important settlement or town which at some time in its history had probably been a royal township. Sutton lathe (which counted as only a half lathe) was based on Sutton-at-Hone and was the only one wholly in west Kent. The lathe of Aylesford (itself a royal manor) stretched from Gravesend and Hoo in the north to Tudeley in the south and to Boughton Malherbe and Frinsted in the east. The half-lathe of Milton centred on the great royal estate of Milton Regis. Wiwart lathe had Wye as its centre; Borowart lathe took its name from the *borough* of Canterbury (just as Burmarsh meant the marsh of the burghers, i.e. the men of Canterbury); Eastry gave its name to a lathe, and the seventh, Limowart lathe, was based on Lyminge. Wye, Eastry and Lyminge are places whose names indicate that they are settlements of great antiquity and it is not surprising therefore to find that at the time of the Conquest they had given their names to three of the major territorial divisions of the county.

For the purposes of raising taxes and of administering justice the lathes (with some boundary changes and alteration of names) remained important units for another six hundred years or so. They still exist, but now have no administrative significance.

The divisions of shires into hundreds was common to all the counties of central, southern and eastern England. According to a not very trustworthy tradition, the division was made by King Alfred. More probably it dates from the 10th century, its purpose being to enable the king to exact the payment due from the county to the royal treasury, and in time of danger to call out the *fyrd*—the Anglo-Saxon equivalent of the 1940 Home Guard. *Hundreds* may have been so called because each was regarded originally as containing nominally one hundred sulungs (hides, as they were termed outside Kent) of land. The hundreds in Kent and in Sussex were much smaller than those in the midland counties; Sussex had more than fifty and Kent, when Domesday Book was compiled, over sixty, whilst Staffordshire, for example, had only five. At the time of the Conquest and for some centuries afterwards each hundred had its own court of law for less important cases, these courts often becoming the private property of great landowners.

The fact that the king now had his own Norman tenants holding great estates, in return for which they owed him military service, did not make the *fyrd* unnecessary. Indeed, within a generation of the Conquest, a Norman king was relying upon his English *levée en masse* to put down his rebellious Norman tenants. The rebellion was the work of Odo, a man of great energy and great ambition, but with little loyalty and less gratitude to his half-brother, the king.

About the year 1082 Odo apparently determined to seek the papacy for himself and began to recruit in England an army of knights to accompany him on an expedition to Italy. He was arrested, and tried, not as bishop of Bayeux (as such he would have been outside the secular jurisdiction) but as earl of Kent. Condemned by the court, Odo was imprisoned in Normandy, but with a number of other important prisoners he was released in 1087 by William on his death-bed. William Rufus restored Odo to his earldom of Kent, but he soon began to cause fresh trouble and many of the Norman barons joined him in rising against the new king. William Rufus took Tonbridge Castle, which was held by Gilbert de Clare, one of Odo's faction, after only two days' siege, but

39 *St Leonard's Tower at West Malling*

40 *Dode manor church. The typical small manor church had been built of wood for centuries, but from the end of the 11th century wood was replaced by stone or flint.*

Pevensey Castle, whither Odo had taken himself, held out for six weeks. When that castle and Odo were finally captured he was taken under escort to Rochester where he was to arrange for the surrender of the castle to the king. However, arriving at Rochester, he managed to give his escort the slip and to join the garrison who were defending the castle there. The king called upon his English subjects for aid in reducing Rochester Castle and it is said that thirty thousand men rallied to him. In the end it was not military force, but the ravages of disease that brought about the capitulation of the castle. Odo was banished from England for ever and his great earldom of Kent came to an end.

The Norman castles of this period were not the buildings that we know today. They were wooden fortresses built on top of an artificial mound called a *motte*. A fine example of a motte is the one at Tonbridge, 40 or 50 ft. high, alongside the stone-built castle which was erected in the 13th century. But a timber fortress is unsatisfactory, incapable of withstanding the assault of battering rams and vulnerable to fire. So, in the 12th century, the timber fortresses began to be replaced by larger structures built of stone. They were too large and too heavy to be sited on the artificial mounds of earth which had supported the earlier wooden castles. Rochester Castle and the keep of Dover Castle, with its walls 20 ft. thick, are amongst the finest examples in the country of Norman castles belonging to the second period. Canterbury Castle is much smaller and more ruinous than the keeps at Dover and Rochester. All three castles, Dover, Canterbury and Rochester, were built during the 12th century for the same obvious purpose, namely to protect the main line of communication between

41 *In the late Norman period masons perfected the craft of stone carving. The south door of Barfreston church is a famous example of the craft*

London and the Continent. Each was probably intended also to serve as a reminder to the townsfolk of the royal power, and as a discouragement to rebellion. Tonbridge Castle, which is somewhat later, was built to keep in order the half-settled Wealden district where communications were still bad—a district which had something in common with the wild marcher lands of the borders of England and Wales where numerous castles were built to enforce law and order. The castles of Dover, Rochester and Tonbridge all figured in the contest between Stephen and Matilda in the years between 1138 and 1142, and in the struggle between John and his barons during the last four years of his life each side sought, by force or by guile, to secure possession of them. Such was their importance to those who aimed to get the royal power into their hands.

The Norman castles at Chilham, Leeds and West Malling (St Leonard's Tower, a beautiful example of a 12th-century keep) were built as strongholds by great landowners. They have not the same strategic significance as Dover, Canterbury, Rochester and Tonbridge, but rather were fortified private residences.

The Normans not only introduced the use of stone in the construction of castles, but also began to build stone churches on a far bigger scale than this country had previously known. The massiveness of Norman church building is perhaps most impressively seen in the great pillars in the crypt of Canterbury Cathedral which carry the weight of the immense structure above; its magnificence in the richly-decorated west doorway of Rochester Cathedral. Many parish churches are Norman, at least in part, and the small church of Barfreston, with its elaborate carving, is as pure an example of late Norman architecture as any county can show. Much of the stone for church-building came from the Caen district of Normandy; its transport is an indication of the Norman gift for efficient organisation. It is an indication also of the prosperity of the county and of the supreme importance which was attached to religion. 'To the men of the twelfth century religion meant a very great deal ... it was not merely for the love of adventure that men in their thousands embarked on the hazardous pilgrimage to the Holy Land; nor was it mere love of splendour that made them build the most magnificent churches that architects of any age could conceive. It was because religion to them was fundamentally the most important, the most real thing. It was the vital force in their lives.'*

* A. L. Poole, *From Domesday Book to Magna Carta*, p.230.

6

Religious Houses

It was because religion had such importance in the Middle Ages that great landowners were prepared to devote part of their wealth to the establishment of monastic houses and that men and women of high rank were prepared to forsake the things of the world, to give themselves up to religion, and to pass their lives within the seclusion of a monastery in performing religious services and in contemplation. The inmates of a religious house lived according to a code of rules of which there were several different varieties, the three most famous being the Benedictine, Cluniac and Cistercian. Orders of canons, the most notable being the Augustinian (or Austin) and Premonstratensian, also had their religious houses with rules somewhat less strict than those of the monks.

42 *The regular life*

The earliest religious houses in Kent, as has already been mentioned, were founded at Canterbury about the year 600 and many more had been established in the eastern part of the county by the end of the eighth century. Several had succumbed to the raids of the Danes. Nearly all, except the two great monasteries at Canterbury, Christ Church (also known as Holy Trinity) and St Augustine's, were at a low ebb when Archbishop Lanfranc began to bring back some organisation into the English Church. At Rochester, for example, Bishop Gundulf in 1089 found that the monastery of St Andrew consisted of only four or five priests, and they were not monks. He caused them to resign and brought in fifty or sixty Benedictines. At Christ Church Lanfranc installed no fewer than 100 Benedictines (a number that by 1125 had risen to 150), most of whom came from Normandy or Burgundy. At Malling Gundulf founded a house for Benedictine nuns about 1090, and a few years later the archbishop refounded for nuns of the same Order the nunnery at Minster-in-Sheppey which for much of the previous 400 years of its existence had suffered repeatedly at the hands of the Danes.

The extent to which religion held men's minds is shown by the number of houses which were founded during the troubled years of Stephen's reign. The king himself, with his queen, Maud, founded a Benedictine abbey at Faversham in 1147, and there he, his wife and his eldest son were buried. At Higham he established a Benedictine nunnery wherein his daughter Mary took her nun's vows; afterwards she became abbess of Romsey. William of Ypres, a professional soldier, founded Boxley Abbey in 1143 at the height of the civil war which was devastating the country, bringing over to occupy it Cistercian monks from

59

43 *Christ Church Cathedral, Canterbury*

Burgundy. About the same time or perhaps a little earlier the great Robert Crevecoeur, who began the building of Leeds Castle, established there a house of Austin Canons, and Richard de Clare, earl of Hereford, who held the Lowy and castle of Tonbridge, founded a similar house near to his stronghold. Somewhat later, in 1178, Richard de Lucy, justiciar of England and the greatest of the king's officers, built a house for Austin Canons at Lessness (Erith) and himself retired to spend his last years there. The Benedictine nunnery at Davington, the Premonstratensian abbeys at St Radegund's (near Dover) and West Langdon, and Combwell Priory (Goudhurst; Austin Canons) all date from the second half of the 12th century. The last Austin Canons' house to be founded in Kent was Bilsington Priory, in 1253.

Besides the great religious houses there were many smaller foundations whose purpose was the charitable one of caring for the sick and the old and providing shelter for pilgrims. Lanfranc founded St John's Hospital at Canterbury

44 *The interior of Christ Church Cathedral, Canterbury*

45 *An 18th-century engraving showing St Bartholomew's Hospital, Rochester*

for infirm or aged men and women about the year 1084; it still continues its good work and so, too, does St Bartholomew's Hospital at Rochester, founded as a hospital for lepers by Bishop Gundulf nearly 900 years ago. Sandwich also has its St Bartholomew's Hospital, a house for elderly men and women, which was established in 1190.

Hospitals, or hostels as perhaps we should call them, for the reception of pilgrims were instituted at Canterbury (Eastbridge Hospital is a good example) and at other places along the route which the pilgrims followed. This was the purpose of the Maison Dieu which the great Hubert de Burgh set up at Dover about 1220 and the Maison Dieu at Ospringe, which Henry III is believed to have founded about 1240, may well have been built with the same object.

Canterbury became a centre of pilgrimage as the result of the murder of Thomas Becket. His quarrel with his erstwhile friend, Henry II, his murder in his own cathedral and his subsequent beatification belong to the history of England and of Christendom. Many stories were told of the miraculous cures effected by the saint. His tomb soon became famed, both in England and overseas, as one of the great places of pilgrimage and the large sums that were offered there show how many men and women made the journey to Canterbury, either following Watling Street like Chaucer's pilgrims from Southwark through Rochester, Sittingbourne, Boughton and Harbledown, or crossing the Strait to Dover and making their way over Barham Downs to the cathedral where the bones of the martyr lay. The Statute of Money of 1335 ordained that pilgrims should enter the country only at the port of Dover, and that tables for the exchange of foreign money should be set up there. The cult of St Thomas continued into the 15th century and in 1420, 250 years after the martyrdom, it was testified by the bailiffs of the city that 100,000 people assembled at Canterbury. The figure must be merely a guess, but obviously great crowds

46 *Miracle at Becket's shrine*

resorted to the shrine in that year. Thereafter the number of pilgrims fell off sharply, and by the 1470s the annual offerings at the shrine were only a pound or two.

The great religious houses had little contact, except as landlords, with the rest of the community. They became a spiritually, and sometimes also physically, comfortable retreat from the cares of the world for the high-born and the well-to-do. Within them, here and there, learning flourished, but for the community at large they did little or nothing. It was a realisation of this, and a realisation of the dreadful lot of the common people, that caused St Francis of Assisi, in Italy, and St Dominic, in Spain, to seek other, less comfortable and more active ways of living the Christian life. Such was the origin of the friars, men who bound themselves to a life of poverty of good works, and of preaching God's word. The first small band of Dominicans reached Canterbury in August 1220. They were cordially received by Archbishop Langton and within a year or so the Blackfriars had been built for their accommodation. Four years later a group of Franciscans, even fewer in number than the Dominicans (there were only nine of them), made their way from Fécamp in Normandy to Canterbury, where five remained whilst the other four set out for London. Thus the friars came to England, a score of men who brought with them a movement that was to affect the religious, the economic, and the social life of the whole country. Their influence and their success were immediate. At Canterbury the Franciscans, or Greyfriars, were given a house and in 1270 they moved to the site and buildings which still go by their name. A few years later a third order of friars, the Carmelites, or Whitefriars, crossed to England and Lord Grey founded the

47 *Chaucer, M.P. for Kent, 1386*

48 *The Friars at Aylesford*

49 *The Fynden gateway to St Augustine's Abbey*

first Carmelite house at Aylesford in the year 1240. In the following year a second was established at Lossenham, in Newenden parish, on the Sussex border.

In the course of time the friars forgot their vows of poverty. As the great monastic houses had done they also grew rich and too fond of the pleasures of the world like Chaucer's friar, 'a wanton and a merry' who 'knew the taverns well in every town'. By the 15th century their best work had been done. Neither friars nor monks were now so essential a part of the religious community; their numbers fell, some of the smaller houses containing only three or five members, and at Davington, in 1535, the priory was entirely deserted. The Black Death of 1349 had struck communal institutions particularly hardly, and after it few religious houses ever again reached their full complement of monks or nuns. That would not have happened if men had still felt monasticism to be a centrally important part of the religious life. When Henry VIII, with Thomas Cromwell as his willing agent, set about dissolving the religious houses in the 1530s he was not therefore attacking an institution still possessed of the vigour of its early years. The king's motives and those of his henchman may have been of the basest, their methods dishonest and their lack of humane consideration for the inmates of suppressed houses sometimes deplorable, but the very fact that the monasteries could be dissolved was a tacit acknowledgement that times and society had changed, that not only had the power of the Crown increased, but also that the religious house was no longer the vital force in men's lives that it had been in earlier centuries.

One effect of the Dissolution was to transfer into lay hands the vast estates owned by the monastic houses. In Kent these estates were especially extensive, the Domesday Book valuation of the lands of Christ Church and St Augustine's, Canterbury, being, together, almost half that of the entire county. As might be expected monastic houses were prudent landlords and capable farmers; from the records which they kept we can learn much about agrarian Kent in the Middle Ages. The next chapter deals with the estates owned by the most wealthy of the Kentish monasteries, Christ Church, Canterbury.

V *Springtime in Canterbury. A branch of the river Stour flows through the Westgate Gardens and by the West Gate, said to have been the first building in the country to have been built specifically to be defended by guns.*

VI *Tonbridge's 13th-century Gatehouse, built into part of the outer bailey walls surrounding the earlier motte and bailey castle, which was itself converted into a shell keep, probably in the late 12th century.*

VII *A lonely outpost on the Romney Marsh. This little church at Fairfield, surrounded by marsh and watercourses and, of course, sheep, was originally a small timber-framed chapel. It contains many treasures, including a three decker pulpit and marvellous old beams.*

VIII *The magnificent 14th-century Perpendicular Gothic west tower of St Mildred, probably the finest in Kent, with its four stages and octagonal corner turrets. Fine views over the town and surrounding areas can be seen from its top.*

7

A Great Medieval Estate

Christ Church Priory acquired most of its estates as gifts from Saxon kings, nobles and thanes. By the time that Domesday Book was compiled the priory had already been in possession of much of its property for two or three hundred years. The estates did not lie together as a compact block, but were scattered over some eight southern counties in England, and the monks also owned land as far away as Ireland. We are concerned here only with their 21 Kentish manors, the situation of which is shown on the map (page 67).* Their total area is not known, but it certainly ran into tens of thousands of acres. The income which the monks derived from their estates was something like two or three thousand pounds a year, although this figure includes the manors which lay outside Kent as well as those within the county. It is impossible to translate these monetary figures into 20th-century terms, but for the Middle Ages they represented vast sums and vast wealth.**

50 *Cellarer: Norman carving at Barfreston*

The typical organisation of a medieval manor in Kent was this: part of the manor, called the *demesne*, belonged in a special sense to the owner, the lord of the manor. He might farm it himself or he might let it out at a fixed annual rent known as a fee-farm, the man who took the demesne on lease being termed the *firmarius* or farmer. For another part of the manor we might use the term *tenant-land*, because it was held by tenants in return for certain services which they owed to the lord of the manor. The tenants also, in a sense, owned the land they occupied; sons succeeded to father and provided that the services were properly performed the tenant could not be turned off his holding. In addition to the demesne and the tenant-land, most manors included pasture, woodland or waste, in all of which the tenants, as well as the lord of the manor, had certain rights.

Some of the priory's manors were many miles from Canterbury, so that it was obviously impossible for the monks to farm their own demesne lands in person. They therefore employed on each manor a manager or bailiff usually known as a serjeant or reeve, to supervise the cultivation of the demesne. He could call upon the tenants to work upon the demesne, and in some counties

* The map also shows the way in which John Boys, writing in 1796, divided the county into four agricultural regions, based approximately on geological formations.

** For a note about the difficulty of assessing the 'purchasing power' of medieval money, see Sir John Clapham's *Concise Economic History of Britain,* p.109, and Lionel Munby, *How Much is that Worth?* (1989)

51 *The ruins of Christ Church Priory*

the greater part of the farm operations was performed by the tenants. It was not so in Kent, where the tenants' services were comparatively light. Often they had to pay small rents, in money or in kind (corn, poultry or eggs), they had to help with the harvest, and they had to perform carrying-services. For the monks, the latter was most important; the lay owner of several manors could move from one to another, living off the produce of each in turn, but the monks had to remain in their cloister at Canterbury, and they had to arrange for the farm-produce to be brought to them. Carrying-service was, therefore, especially useful to a monastery situated, as Christ Church was, at a distance from some of its estates. Nevertheless, the lord of the manor frequently found it more convenient to exchange (or *commute*) his tenants' services for a small fixed yearly rent in money.

The amount of help which the monks could demand from their tenants in cultivating the demesne was, in any case, trifling, and it was necessary to employ a large number of paid agricultural labourers, who lived on the estate, and by whom most of the work on the farm was done. For example, at Monkton in 1307 there was a permanent full-time staff of 34 which included:

17 ploughmen	3 stackers
4 shepherds	3 drovers
2 cowherds	1 lambherd
1 swineherd	1 sower
1 harrower	1 cheesemaker

Their wages were about 3s. a year, together with food, and some of them received a gift of gloves once a year. In addition, there were the serjeant (£2 14s. 10d. a year), the hayward (£1 14s. 1d. a year), and the beadle (13s. 4d.

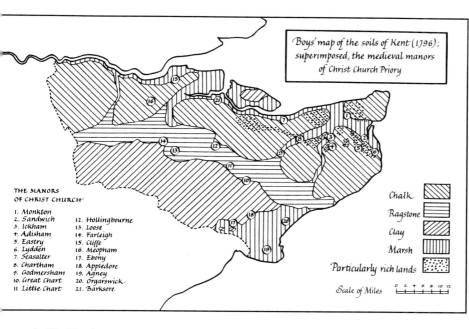

Boys' map of the soils of Kent (1796); superimposed, the medieval manors of Christ Church Priory

THE MANORS OF CHRIST CHURCH

1. Monkton
2. Sandwich
3. Ickham
4. Adisham
5. Eastry
6. Lydden
7. Seasalter
8. Chartham
9. Godmersham
10. Great Chart
11. Little Chart
12. Hollingbourne
13. Loose
14. Farleigh
15. Cliffe
16. Meopham
17. Ebony
18. Appledore
19. Agney
20. Orgarswick
21. Barksore

Chalk
Ragstone
Clay
Marsh
Particularly rich lands
Scale of Miles

year). Hollingbourne was a smaller manor, employing only eight ploughmen, a shepherd, a swineherd, an oxherd, a cowherd, a goatherd and a dairymaid, with wages at more than twice the rates that were paid at Monkton.

The lord of the manor enjoyed another source of profit in that he was entitled to hold a court, at which his tenants were bound to appear, and the fees and fines of which went into his pocket. On some manors the lord had much more extensive rights of jurisdiction than on others, depending, in theory, on the extent of the grant from the King, but depending much more, in practice, upon the custom of the particular manor. The monks of Christ Church had fairly wide rights; they were entitled, for example, to have their own gaol (even that was a source of profit), they were entitled to treasure-trove and to a share in wrecks driven ashore on their land; they could fine their tenants who brewed bad beer or sold bread under weight; and all ordinary civil actions in which their tenants were involved must be settled in the manorial court.

This was the kind of organisation which existed on the manors of a great monastery, but a manor belonging to a lay landlord would be organised in the same way. No doubt the monks were, in general, more businesslike and efficient than other owners; they preserved their records (hence our knowledge of their affairs) and there was a continuity of policy from one generation to the next which was often lacking on other manors. But, in their standard of living, the Prior of Christ Church could be compared with one of the great barons, and the monks with his squires. In the matter of food, they looked after themselves well; one Trinity Sunday, about 1190, Giraldus Cambrensis, who was visiting the priory, counted 16 courses at dinner. Fish, eggs, poultry, cheese and bread were the principal foods. The monks' bread was always wheaten, but the servants had to be content with bread of barley or mixed corn. The rule of the priory forbade the eating of meat, but this came to mean that meat could be eaten anywhere except in the refectory, and large quantities of beef, mutton and pork were consumed. Beer was the staple drink, but the best French wines were also imported through Sandwich. Between the years 1100 and 1400 the number of monks varied from 30 to 150, with an average of 60 to 80. Their servants numbered more than twice as many as the monks themselves, so the total household was usually well over 200. In addition, there were numerous and often important guests to be fed. These figures give some idea of the size of the problem which confronted the cellarer, whose business it was to provide the monks with food and drink, and to look after the guests and pilgrims.

Against this background of manorial and monastic organisation, we can examine the ups and downs which the Christ Church estates underwent between the 12th century and the 16th, when the monastery was dissolved.

During the latter part of the 11th century, it had already become quite usual for the priory to let off its demesne lands rather than for the monks to farm them themselves. In this way the monastery's income from rents was increased, but the large quantities of food which were required for the sustenance of the monks and their numerous servants had to be bought in the market. This was sound economy so long as prices remained low, as they did throughout the 12th century. However, by about the year 1225 the prices of corn and of cattle had risen so much that it began to pay the monks to farm their own lands and grow their own food rather than to let off the demesnes for money-rents.

The century from 1225 to 1325 saw demesne-farming at its most prosperous. Crop-growing became so profitable that a good deal of pasture was broken up and converted into arable. The monks were progressive farmers; they manured their lands thoroughly; they dressed the heavy clay lands with chalk or lime; they knew that it was better for each farm to get seedcorn from another farm than to use home-grown seed; and they discovered that it paid to sow corn seed rather more thickly than was customary at that time. At Barksore, near Chatham, for example, wheat was sown at the rate of four bushels to the acre, and at Monkton the rate for oats was seven bushels, and for barley six bushels to the acre. Where land had been recently manured and dressed, a bushel of seed could be expected to give a crop of four-and-a-half bushels, but if the land had not been treated the return was likely to be not more than three-and-a-half bushels. To manure the land sheep were folded on the upland fields, as they still are, but the main source of manure was the farmyard. Great numbers of cattle were kept, and to feed them (as well as to make pottage and coarse bread for the lower ranks of servants) peas and beans were increasingly grown from about 1275 onwards.

By 1322 the monks had nearly 5,000 acres of land under cultivation in Kent, growing the following crops:

53 *Mowing*

Wheat	1,312	acres
Barley	981	acres
Oats	1,223	acres
Peas and beans	1,210	acres
Rye	52	acres
Total	4,779	acres

In other counties, where the soil was poorer, a much larger proportion of their land was under rye. Barley, to which nearly 1,000 acres was devoted, was used almost wholly for brewing beer.

Pasture was skilfully combined with arable farming. Huge flocks of sheep were kept, the Monkton estate, for example, carrying 2,000 head of sheep in 1322. In all, in that year, the monks had some 10,000 sheep on their Kentish manors. They were kept mainly for their wool, which was exported through Sandwich, New Romney and Rochester, but they also ensured a good supply of mutton, and cheese was made from the ewes' milk (10 or 12 ewes were regarded as equivalent to one cow). From dairy-farming, cheese was much more in demand than milk or butter. In one year the farm at Monkton produced almost a ton of cheese. This is all the more remarkable when it is remembered that there were no artificial foods to enrich the cows' milk in the winter, and that the cheese-making season lasted only from April until September.

In the first few years of the 14th century Kentish agriculture prospered as never before. Corn was being sold off the Christ Church demesnes, not only in the local markets, but also in London and abroad, the main port of export being Sandwich. These figures for the manors of Agney (in Romney Marsh) and Ickham shows how much the income from corn sales increased in a period of 35 years:

	Agney	Ickham
1280	£10	£15
1315	£49	£28

Similarly, the profits from the sale of wool from all the Kentish manors, which had been £48 in 1288, went up to £146 in 1321 and to £157 in 1322.

And then came one of those sudden reversals in fortune which have always marked the history of agriculture. In 1323 the profits from wool sales were down to £93, and they never again reached £100. Corn production fell, and farming, which had been so prosperous until about 1320, 10 years later was in a sorry plight.

What were the causes of this sudden decline? The weather was certainly one of them. Towards the end of the 13th century and during the early 14th, Kent suffered from a series of severe storms which must have made farming difficult. More serious still were droughts during the 1320s, followed by pestilence which carried off a great part of the sheep and cattle. At the same time the sea flooded the low-lying parts of the manors near the coast—Monkton the River Wantsum still flowed on the south and west sides of the Isle of Thanet, and Monkton therefore was subject to flooding by the sea), Lydden (in Worth parish) and Ebony, Agney and Orgarswick on Romney Marsh. From these causes the monks lost, in the years 1324-6, no fewer than 4,585 of their 10,000 sheep. Indeed, except on Romney Marsh, the flocks never recovered nor did sheep-rearing ever again reach its former importance and prosperity. Dairy farming also suffered; the profits for 1350, for example, were half those for 1320, and they continued to fall for the rest of the 14th century.

Before the agricultural economy could recover from the damage caused by flood, storms, drought and pestilence, it was further weakened by the Black

54   *Sheep shearing*

Death of 1348-9. The plague struck west Kent more severely than the eastern part of the county, and altogether wiped out some villages, such as Dode (near Snodland). A monk of Canterbury, writing at the time, said that the pestilence 'left barely a third part of mankind alive', but that must have been an exaggeration; more probably about a third part died, although some places were stricken more hardly than their neighbours, and the bishop of Rochester for example, seems to have lost the whole of his household of 32 men.

One result of the Black Death was that the number of farm labourers was much reduced and those who survived naturally pressed for higher wages. In the hundred years between 1310 and 1410 the average wage went up from 3s. 0d. to about 18s. 0d. a year. Because labour was more costly, the monks, during the second half of the 14th century, began to require the tenants to perform their labour-services, instead of commuting them for money, but the brunt of the work on the priory's farms continued to be borne by labourers hired for wages.

Reference has already been made to the damage which the low-lying manors near the sea suffered from storms and floods. To protect them sea-walls had to be built and ditches cut, and they must constantly be kept in repair. This applied particularly to the great tract of land lying between Hythe and Rye which comprises Romney Marsh, Walland Marsh, Denge Marsh and Guldeford Level. It embraces more than 50,000 acres of some of the most fertile land in the whole country, marsh only in name, nearly all of it lying below sea-level. The Marsh has evolved from estuarine swamp during the last 2,000 years as a result partly of natural causes and partly of man's efforts. Its history is complicated, too long and too confusing to be described here in any detail. The south-western boundary of Romney Marsh proper follows the line of the Rhee Wall, now an earth embankment flanked by dykes that stretches from Appledore to New Romney. South-west of the Rhee much of the land was owned by the archbishops of Canterbury, by whom it was reclaimed from the sea in the 12th and 13th centuries, the 'innings' bearing the names of successive archbishops— St Thomas, Baldwin, Boniface and Pecham. These newly-reclaimed lands proved richly fertile, once the soil had been dressed and manured, and they could be let off at high rents.

Because the greater part of the Marsh lies below sea-level, every landowner however far from the sea his own land may lie, is concerned in the preservation of the sea-wall and the maintenance of the dykes. From a very early date a special system of local government was evolved to deal with the upkeep of the walls and dykes. Twenty-four lawful and sworn men of Romney Marsh were chosen to keep them in repair, the sworn men having the right to levy a scot, or tax, upon every landowner in the Marsh. This scheme had been in existence 'from time immemorial' when it was confirmed by Henry III in 1252. Later, the scheme which had been worked out by the marshmen was adopted in other parts of the country where low-lying lands had to be protected against flood.

However, the walls and dykes were inadequate to defend the Marsh from ravages of the unusually severe storms of the latter part of the 13th and the beginning of the 14th centuries. In 1284, so Camden recorded 300 years later, 'the sea driven by violent winds overwhelmed this tract and made great havoc

of men, cattle and buildings, and having destroyed the little populous village of Promhill [which stood between Dungeness and Rye] changed the channel of the Rother, which here [at New Romney] emptied itself into the sea and filled up its mouth, making it a new and shorter course by Rye'. We shall have to say something more about these catastrophic changes in the topography of the Marsh when we come to the history of the Cinque Ports. They obviously cast a heavy burden on those who, like the monks of Christ Church, owned land there. Not merely did the monks pay the common scot, but they also spent large sums of money privately on cutting new dykes, and building and repairing walls, usually of clay but sometimes strengthened with timber, straw or turf to protect their lands against inundation. Similar work had to be carried out on the Thanet and Thames-side marshes, although not on anything like the same scale—there are no items of expenditure to compare with the £1,500 which was spent on the 'inning' of Appledore marsh during the 15th century.

We must rapidly pass over the history of the Christ Church estates during the last 150 years before the Dissolution. After the disasters of the 14th century agriculture gradually recovered during the 15th, although it did not again reach the heights of prosperity of the years 1280 to 1320. As it recovered, the monks began to change their policy and, instead of themselves farming their demesne lands, they let off entire manors on long leases, thus ensuring for themselves a large income from rents and freedom from trouble in the management of their estates. They lived the comfortable life of well-to-do landowners, but they also spent a great deal of money on the cathedral. The latter-day monks may not for the most part have been pious men, but they were good husbandmen, and their Priors Selling and Goldstone built the great Angel Steeple, or Bell

Harry, surely the loveliest cathedral tower in England. Such conspicuous expenditure suggests that Kentish agriculture, by the end of the 15th century, was recovering something of its former prosperity.

This chapter is based almost entirely on the records of Christ Church Priory. For privately-owned estates no such records are available, but (allowing for the fact that monks were among the best and most progressive farmers of their time) what is true of the Christ Church manors would no doubt hold for other estates in the county. We can, then, sum up the history of agriculture in Kent during the Middle Ages by saying that 1100 to 1280 was a period of steadily increasing prosperity; the years from 1280 to 1320 saw agriculture at its peak; there followed a sudden and sharp decline, the slump lasting until after the middle of the century; from about 1370 onwards a slow recovery set in, continuing during the 15th century, but the levels of the 'high-farming' period of 1280 to 1320 were never again reached during the Middle Ages.

8

Risings in Kent

Discontents in the generation following the Black Death finally culminated in the Rising of 1381. The Rising began in the south-east of England, and amongst the ring-leaders men from Kent were numerous. Its causes were various and to some extent are likely to remain obscure. The 1380s were not a time of great hardship; wages, as we have already seen, had risen; in spite of attempts by Parliament in the Statute of Labourers of 1351 to keep them stationary. Because wages had risen and labour was scarce, there was a tendency for landlords to require their tenants to perform labour-services, instead of commuting them for money payments, and no doubt this was unpopular. Serfs, increasingly, were becoming dissatisfied with their status, and an Act of Parliament in 1377 provided for commissions to be set up to inquire into the misbehaviour of villeins and land-tenants towards their lords, a clear indication that there had been trouble. However, serfdom was rare in Kent, and labour-services were always light, so discontent on these two scores is not likely to have been a salient factor in the county. Certainly the king's long-drawn-out war against France was unpopular, partly because the war was costly, and partly because it was not going well, the French on several occasions raiding and pillaging towns and villages on the Kent and Sussex coasts and even along the Thames estuary as far up as Gravesend. To pay for the war the government resorted to a poll-tax, payable by every man and woman over the age of 15, genuine beggars alone excepted. The poll-tax, which was levied on several occasions, does not seem to have been unfair; it was carefully graduated, so that the great and wealthy John of Gaunt paid 520 times as much as a labourer, but like all new taxes it was detested. Finally, there was a feeling of unrest, of refusal to accept the existing state of things, which was perhaps the natural aftermath of such a catastrophe as the Black Death. It was in this spirit that John Ball, known as the mad priest of Kent, went round the county preaching on the theme:

> When Adam delved and Evé span,
> Who was then the gentleman?

until the archbishop of Canterbury put him under lock and key in his gaol at Maidstone.

The rising in Kent began in the early summer of 1381 at Dartford where, according to an unsubstantiated legend, a tax-collector insulted the daughter of

57 *John Ball*

73

a worthy townsman, who promptly knocked out his brains. Walter Tyler, who was possibly born in Kent and who may at one time have been a soldier, crossed to Kent from Essex, where he had already been involved in an insurrection, and put himself at the head of those Kentish men who rose in support of the townsman of Dartford. Rochester Castle was attacked, and the garrison was compelled to release a number of prisoners lodged there. Tyler then advanced to Maidstone, and there freed John Ball from the archbishop's prison. The next we hear of him is at Canterbury, which was at the mercy of the mob for the greater part of June. Sir William Septvans, the high sheriff of the county, was seized, and he was compelled to deliver up all his official records, which were at once burnt.

58 *The* Wat Tyler, *a fine old timber-framed inn at Dartford, claims to be the 1377 home of Wat Tyler.*

Without them the sheriff could not organise the tax-collection. Elsewhere also, at Manston, at Gillingham, at Petham and at Wye, the rioters destroyed records, probably manorial documents which recorded the labour services and rents which each tenant owed to his lord. This is some evidence as to the nature of the discontents which, in part, gave rise to the revolt. To the same effect is the record of a riot at Margate on 24 June, when the rioters (almost certainly they were tenants of St Augustine's, Canterbury) determined that they would no longer perform their customs and services and threatened to cut off the heads of any of their fellow-tenants who did so.

The story of the meeting, at London, between Walter Tyler with, it is said, 100,000 rebels at his back, and the young King Richard II is well known. On the faith of the king's promise the rioters returned home, but when the king afterwards went back on his word, there were further risings in Kent, especially in the Weald during the month of September.

Many of the rioters were subsequently prosecuted, and the official records show that the summer risings were widespread. At each of the following towns and villages it was alleged that people were slain, houses pulled down, property stolen or men compelled to hand over their money: Margate, Manston, Monkton, Ickham, Canterbury, Petham, Waltham, Chillenden, Wootton, Boughton Aluph, Wye, Kennington, Willesborough, Mersham, Stalisfield, Throwley, Boughton-under-Blean, Preston-next-Faversham, Ospringe, Teynham, Borden, Gillingham, Chatham, Rochester, Maidstone, Staplehurst, Tenterden and Appledore. The September revolt seems to have been limited to the country south of Maidstone— Loose, Linton, Farleigh, Hunton, Staplehurst, Cranbrook, Biddenden and Frittenden. It is noticeable that the riots were often caused by men who are recorded as coming from another parish, and as having no lands or goods.

The places named in the records as being the scene of enormities committed by the insurrectionists during the summer all lie to the east of the Medway, although two of the malefactors are described as of Erith and Malling respectively. It seems improbable that the insurrection, which is supposed to have begun at Dartford, did not affect the area west of the Medway and the apparent passivity of west Kent is more likely due to the loss of official records than to any natural inclination towards decorous behaviour on the part of Kentishmen compared with Men of Kent.*

In spite of John Ball's association with the Rising, it does not seem that religious discontents were among the causes of it. Nevertheless, dissatisfaction with the Church was fairly widespread in the second half of the 14th century, and Wycliffe became the leader of a movement for reform. His followers were known as 'Lollards', one of the most prominent of whom was Sir John Oldcastle. The Lollard rising of 1414 was a small affair and easily put down; the reason for mentioning it is that Oldcastle lived at Cooling Castle, a fortified manor-house built by Lord Cobham towards the end of the 14th century. It is likely that Cobham was granted royal permission to fortify his manor-house because Cooling lies in the Thames-side marshes where the danger of raids by the French had to be guarded against. Indeed, in 1380 Gravesend had been plundered by the French and many of the townspeople carried off, it was said, into slavery.

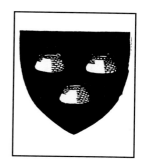

59 *Arms of Septvans*

Cade's Rebellion in 1450 was a more serious rising, with national as well as local features. It occurred against the background of rivalry and strife which five years later were to erupt into the Wars of the Roses. Cade himself (that may or may not have been his name; at other times he called himself John Mortimer, suggestive of a connection with the family of the great earls of March) claimed that he had been born in Ireland, and had served as a soldier under the duke of York.

The rebellion began in late May, when Cade encamped with his followers at Blackheath. They were not an undisciplined rabble but an organised military force. On the approach of the king's forces they withdrew through Bromley towards Sevenoaks, probably intending to attack Knole, the seat of Lord Say, Constable of Dover Castle, who was hated in Kent as a severe and notorious extortioner. The royal forces followed the rebels and at Solefields, near Sevenoaks, they clashed, Sir Humphrey Stafford, the royalist leader, and 24 of his men being killed. When the defeat and the unreliability of the army became known, the king fled to Kenilworth, leaving London at the mercy of the rebels. For three days they were masters of the City, taking Say out of the Tower and executing him along with his son-in-law who had been sheriff of Kent. Then the citizens drove the rebels across the river to Southwark where they lay encamped, the bridge closed against them. Though no longer in control of the City they remained a formidable force, and the King's Council now expressed its readiness to receive the Kentish 'Complaint' and to secure a pardon for all those who would peaceably go to their homes. The Complaint listed a number

* On the usual assumption that those who live east of the Medway are Men of Kent, and Kentish Men who live west of the river.

*60 Cooling Castle's
great entrance gate*

of discontents, such as the misgovernment of the country, the maladministration
of justice, and the losses in Normandy, which affected the whole of the kingdom,
but others were peculiar to Kent. The people of Kent, for example, feared, or
said they feared, that they were to be punished because when the impeached
and exiled earl of Suffolk was in flight from Ipswich to the Continent in the
preceding April, he had been taken off his ship by some Kentishmen, beheaded
at sea, and his body cast on the shore at Dover. They also complained that Lord
Say and others had acted oppressively, and that elections of the Knights of the
Shire were accompanied by intimidation and bribery. Another complaint casts
an interesting sidelight on travelling conditions in the county at that time; the
men of west Kent said that they had to attend the Sessions at Canterbury
'which causeth to some men five days' journey'.

The offer of a free pardon was accepted, and the rebellion collapsed. Cade
himself did not give up the struggle, perhaps because the pardon granted to him
was made out in the name of John Mortimer, and was therefore of no force.
With a few followers he fled first to Dartford, then to Rochester. He tried,
unsuccessfully, to capture Queenborough Castle. From there he escaped into
the Weald, crossed the Sussex border, and two or three days later was killed
at Heathfield. William Parmynter, a smith of Faversham, tried to take over the
leadership of the few remaining rebels and he was not caught until the winter.
He lacked Cade's ability, and there was never again any serious danger after
the middle of July. The Rebellion, in fact, lasted just about one month.

The list of those to whom pardons were granted is still extant. It shows that Cade had some hundreds of followers in Kent, that they came predominantly from west Kent and the Weald, and that they belonged to the middle and upper ranks of society, including one knight, 18 esquires, 74 gentlemen and numerous yeomen. In this respect Cade's Rebellion differed from the Rising of 1381, which was the work of the peasantry, artisans and labourers.

By Letters Patent dated 1 August 1450 a commission was appointed to investigate divers trespasses and extortions committed in the county. The Commission, which included amongst others the two archbishops and the duke of Buckingham, quickly got to work. It was not concerned with the events of Cade's rising but with the illegalities and extortions committed earlier, to which the Kentishmen referred in their Complaint. It seems that the rebels were not without their sympathisers amongst the factions that surrounded the king. A minor and unsuccessful revolt in 1452 under the leadership of John Wilkins, about whom practically nothing is known was almost certainly a local manifestation of the rivalry of the dukes of York and Somerset. According to the subsequent indictment of the rebels, they claimed that Cade was still alive and that he was their chief captain, an example of the notorious reluctance of insurgents to believe in the death of their leader. But in a time of such confusion almost any rumour was likely to find acceptance somewhere.

61 *St Dunstan's, Cranbrook*

62 *Knole: the Bourchier Gateway*

9

The Cinque Ports

As has previously been said, the position of Kent, lying as it does between London and the continent, gave it an exceptional importance in the Middle Ages. The towns on the Kent coast enjoyed a corresponding importance, since they were at once the ports through which most of the continental traffic passed, and also England's first line of defence against invasion from France or Flanders. The king dealt with Hastings, Romney, Hythe, Dover and Sandwich in the same way as he dealt with his great baronial landowners; each town was assigned certain duties to be performed when demanded by the king, and in return each was granted certain privileges. It was a normal arrangement within the feudal system.

The five towns, together with Rye and Winchelsea (both of them, like Hastings, lying in Sussex) formed a group known as the Cinque Ports and the Two Antient Towns, which was without parallel in England. From the 12th century onward the Ports had their own system of courts and meetings, and they worked together as a confederation which, for some purposes, was independent of the counties in which the ports lay. They were at the zenith of their power at the end of the 13th and the beginning of the 14th century—the exact period when Kentish agriculture also was at its zenith, although there is only a loose connection between the prosperity of agriculture and the prosperity of the ports. Soon afterwards they were in decline, but one of their special privileges, 'Honours at Court', they retain to the present day.

The Domesday Book entries for Dover, Sandwich and Romney, which are referred to in Chapter Five, record that ship-service was already being performed in the reign of King Edward the Confessor. The ships which the towns had to provide for the king's use were quite small, each carrying a crew of 21 men. They might be used either to ferry the king, his men and his goods across the Channel, or to repel pirates. There were no such things as separate passenger ships, cargo ship and warships—the same vessel at different times might be all three. The Bayeux tapestry contains several illustrations of ships of this period.

William the Conqueror no doubt continued the ports in their privileged position, and in 1155 and 1156 Henry II granted them charters confirming their special rights. Like many other towns, they were granted exemption from taxation, and each town had authority to set up its own court of law, independent of the shire court. In addition, the ports were granted two other privileges: the

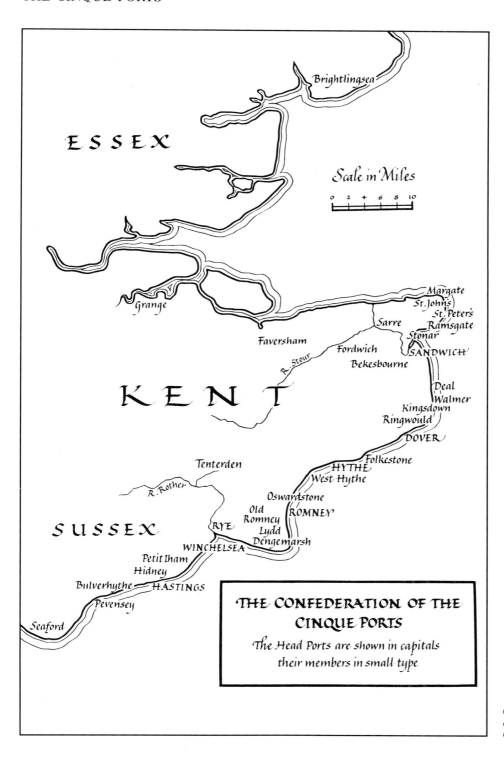

Scale in Miles

ESSEX

Brightlingsea

Grange

Faversham

Margate
St.Johns
Sarre
St.Peter's
Ramsgate
Stonar
SANDWICH

Fordwich
Bekesbourne

R. Stour

KENT

Deal
Walmer
Kingsdown
Ringwould

DOVER

Tenterden

R. Rother

Folkestone
HYTHE
West Hythe

Oswardstone
Old Romney
Lydd
Dengemarsh

ROMNEY

SUSSEX

RYE

WINCHELSEA

Petit Iham
Hidney
Bulverhythe — HASTINGS
Pevensey
Seaford

THE CONFEDERATION OF THE CINQUE PORTS

The Head Ports are shown in capitals
their members in small type

63 *Map showing the confederation of the Cinque Ports*

64 *Seal of Faversham,* regno *Edward I*

first, 'Honours at Court', was the privilege of holding the canopy over the king and queen at the coronation; the second, 'den and strond', was the right for fishermen from the ports to land on the shore at Great Yarmouth in order to sell their catch and dry their nets. A relic of the first privilege still exists in that representatives of the Cinque Ports occupy special seats in Westminster Abbey during the coronation service. The right of 'den and strond' was more valuable than might at first sight appear. Fishing was one of the main industries of coastal towns, upon which their prosperity in part depended. The North Sea was the great fishing ground, but unless catches could be landed and sold quickly, the fish was likely to be bad and unsaleable by the time it was brought ashore. Yarmouth was much nearer to the fishing-grounds than the Kent ports were and, moreover, it served East Anglia which, in the Middle Ages, contained the most prosperous and the most populous counties in England.

Not all of the ports' activities were so innocent as fishing. The portsmen were constantly at enmity with the men of Yarmouth, and their quarrel reached a head in 1297. When, in that year, the king's fleet, which included contingents from Yarmouth and from the Cinque Ports, was on its way to Sluys, England at that time being at war with France, the portsmen fell upon the Yarmouth ships, destroying 32 of them and killing over 200 of their crews. But even such an outrageous act of indiscipline as this the king was powerless to punish. The Cinque Ports also carried on what were really private wars with a number of foreign ports, as well as maintaining a feud with Fowey and some other ports in the west of England. It would, of course, be unfair to lay the blame for this state of affairs entirely upon the Cinque Ports. Probably they were no worse, and no better, than their opponents.

Henry II's charters of 1155 and 1156 were granted to the ports individually, not as a confederation. Nevertheless, the confederation was already in existence, in at least a rudimentary form, by the middle of the 12th century, because the Court of Shepway, the common court of all the ports, originated not later than 1150. It took its name from the Lathe of Shepway, the Lathe which included south-east Kent. For the Cinque Ports it was very much what the Shire Court was for the county. To the portsmen it must have been a great advantage to have their own court, and to be exempt from the obligation of attending the Shire Court at Penenden Heath. The Warden of the Cinque Ports (an offce which from the time of Edward I has always been combined with that of Constable of Dover Castle) had the same kind of authority over the ports that the sheriff had had over the rest of the county. He was a royal officer and was appointed by the king, but on his appointment he took an oath to uphold the privileges of the Cinque Ports. He was, therefore, the ports' representative and protector, as well as the king's representative. In course of time the ports found it convenient to establish other courts—the court of Brodhill, and the court of Guestling, which later became one court known as the Brotherhood and Guestling, and which still occasionally meets. By the 20th century the term 'court' has come to mean, usually, a place where lawsuits are decided and criminals are punished. The Court of Shepway, the Brotherhood and Guestling, were courts in that sense, but they were mainly concerned with non-legal affairs, meeting to transact the common business of

65 *Many of the country's greatest people have served the king as Lord Warden. Here is Sir Winston Churchill when he was installed at a Court of Shepway in 1946*

66 *The cross above the Marsh, on the hilltop near Lympne, which marks the ancient site of the place where, in medieval times, the senior court of the Cinque Ports was held*

the ports. In fact, they should be thought of as being more akin to the modern county council than a court of law. This mixture of judicial and administrative functions continued to be characteristic of local government bodies in England until the 19th century.

To us today the casualness with which the unique constitutional structure of the Cinque Ports emerged during the course of a century or two, without any royal proclamation, still less any Act of Parliament, must seem surprising. Equally surprising is the way in which, without any authority from the king, the Cinque Ports brought other towns and villages, known as limbs or members, into their confederation, to share their burdens and some of their privileges. Rye and Wiinchelsea in this way were at first attached to Hastings, but grew into towns of such importance that later they ceased to be mere limbs of Hastings, and became known as the Two Ancient Towns of Rye and Winchelsea. The map on page 79 shows the various members of the Cinque Ports in the 17th century. In some cases the reason for the association between a member and its Head Port is obvious: thus Rye was the nearest port to Tenterden (which had its harbour at Smallhythe, literally 'small harbour', where Henry V had built men-of war), Lydd was near Romney, and Ramsgate and Deal were nearest to Sandwich; Grange (part of Gillingham) and Bekesbourne (near Canterbury) were connected with Hastings because they happened to be owned by men who also held land at Hastings. However, in other cases, the reason for the attachment of one of the more distant members to its Head Port is not clear.

For the century and a half from the Conquest until the year 1204, when King John lost Normandy, the ports were for the most part engaged in the peaceful pursuits of fishing, trade, and ferrying men and goods across to the Continent. Sandwich was the main port of trade, Dover for passage to the Continent. Of other, less peaceful, pursuits, the main one was piracy. Many complaints were made of the behaviour of the portsmen and more than once the king was obliged to compensate foreign merchants whom they had attacked. The loss of Normandy in 1204 gave the Cinque Ports a new importance in the defence of the country. In 1217 their fleet, in a battle off Sandwich, defeated the much larger French fleet bringing reinforcements to Louis of France, who was then endeavouring to seize the throne of England. Louis gave up the attempt and Henry III, who had succeeded King John on his death in 1216, began his long and troubled reign. The Barons' War, which disturbed Henry III's later years, saw both sides trying to win the support of the ports. On the whole they favoured the party of Simon de Montfort, but his defeat at Evesham in 1265 does not seem to have affected them much. Winchelsea was admonished by Prince Edward for adhering to de Montfort, but no other punishment followed. The ports were still too necessary to the safety of the realm for the king to risk alienating them by any unwise disciplinary moves. Indeed only a dozen years later Edward I granted to the Confederation the first of the great charters which codified their privileges and duties, and the fact that it was granted to the ports collectively strengthened the corporate spirit of the Confederation.

However, by the 14th century the heyday of the Cinque Ports was passing. The king's government was becoming increasingly powerful, and unwilling to

brook independence on the part of any group of towns. Sea-going ships were becoming larger, and the contribution which the Cinque Ports could make towards the king's navy was ceasing to have so great an importance. The French, who for more than a century had suffered at the hands of the portsmen, now turned the tables on them and began to harry the Kent and Sussex coasts. At Dover a wall was built to protect the town (Townwall Street marks the line of it), and at Sandwich the earthen ramparts, which now make a pleasant promenade around part of the town, were thrown up. Hythe was too poor to afford any protective works and indeed Henry IV had to agree to remit the burgesses' service in order to dissuade them from abandoning their town altogether. The ports which were now prospering were those like Southampton, London, King's Lynn and Boston, whose fortunes were soundly based on trade, not like the Cinque Ports, on fishing, with occasional acts of piracy. In 1572 it was recorded that, in the whole of England, there were 135 ships of 100 tons and upwards; only one belonged to a Kent port, namely, Dover. The extent to which the importance of the ports had declined is shown by the very small contingent which they contributed to the fleet which was to defend England against the Spanish Armada—a danger that was so serious as to call for the country's greatest effort. All that the Cinque Ports could send was seven small ships—the *Elnathan* or *Elizabeth* of Dover (120 tons), the *Reuben* of Sandwich (110 tons), the *William* of Rye (80 tons), the *Ann Bonaventure* of

Hastings (70 tons), the *John* of Romney (60 tons), the *Grace of God* of Hythe (50 tons) and the *Hazard* of Faversham (38 tons).

The final cause in the decline of the ports was the change which the Kentish coast-line underwent in the later Middle Ages. In the chapter on the estates of Christ Church Priory reference is made to the changes which took place on Romney Marsh, including the great storm of 1284 which caused the Rother to change its course, so that it flowed into the sea at Rye, leaving Romney haven high and dry. At Hythe the action of the sea built up a great bar of shingle so that the old town of Hythe is now a mile away from the shore. The harbour at Dover silted up and its site is covered by shops, streets and houses; a new harbour had to be constructed, but it required constant effort to keep it clear. At Sandwich the river Wantsum and the harbour were being encroached upon by banks of sand. In the 16th century an Italian merchant-ship sank in the harbour and the sand banked up around it, almost blocking the channel. Thus, by the 17th century, the confederation of the Cinque Ports retained only its outward forms of power and privilege; in truth its day had passed. Their past grandeur and subsequent decline are both recalled in Rudyard Kipling's felicitous description of them as 'ports of stranded pride'.

68 *The Common Seal of the town and port of Folkestone*

10

Other Towns in the Middle Ages

Apart from Dover, Sandwich, Hythe and New Romney, the other Kent towns of some size in the Middle Ages were, first and foremost, Canterbury, followed at a considerable distance by Rochester, Faversham, Maidstone, Cranbrook, Tonbridge and Gravesend. Most of them were important as centres of communication. At Canterbury the roads from Lympne, Dover, Richborough and Reculver met, and Watling Street crossed the River Stour. Faversham lay just to the north of Watling Street, beside the Creek with its useful harbour. At Rochester, like Canterbury of importance since Roman times, a bridge carried Watling Street across the River Medway. Gravesend developed as a centre of communication because, water transport being quicker and easier than transport by road, most passengers and goods from or into Kent were carried by river between London and Gravesend. Maidstone stood at the point where the east-west road crossed the Medway, and where it intercepted the road running southward from Rochester into the Weald. The town of Tonbridge grew up around the castle which guarded the river crossing. The only town that owed its importance primarily to industry was Cranbrook.

69 *The Old Market House, Sevenoaks*

Each of the larger towns was a market for the surrounding countryside. Canterbury had markets on two days in the week, and like Maidstone held four fairs a year. Several smaller towns also had weekly markets, including St Mary Cray, Dartford, Wrotham, Sevenoaks, Malling, Milton Regis, Lenham and Ashford. All the towns, even a city such as Canterbury which was the ecclesiastical capital of England, owed much of their prosperity to the fertility and richness of the countryside in which they were situated. Places like Bexley and Chislehurst, now densely populated, were insignificant villages in the Middle Ages because the soil was too poor to support a prosperous agricultural industry. Even in the largest towns no man was far removed from the land and many of the townsmen worked on their fields just outside the town itself.

Towns fitted somewhat uneasily into the feudal order of things. Some, such as Canterbury, Dover and Rochester, managed to get themselves accepted virtually as tenants-in-chief, that is, the burgesses held their town directly from the king in return for an annual fee-farm rent, and thus avoided subjection to any manorial lord. To the townspeople such an arrangement was both profitable and convenient.

85

70 *Tonbridge, an ancient town which grew up around the old castle and the crossings over the river Medway*

Some towns succeeded in obtaining from the Crown the grant of valuable privileges and exemptions. As noticed in the last chapter, Henry II granted charters to certain of the Cinque Ports. Canterbury received a charter during the same reign, and Rochester and Faversham were granted charters by Henry III. The burgesses of these towns, like those of the Cinque Ports, were to be free of tax or duty wherever they traded in England. They were authorised to establish their own civil courts so that such legal actions as those concerned with land or with debts could be determined locally and the townsmen were exempted from attendance at the Shire Court. Serious criminal cases were still reserved for trial by the king's judges when they came to take the county assizes two or three times a year, but the town itself, and not the sheriff, was made responsible for apprehending criminals. And when taxes and subsidies had to be raised, the towns themselves collected their contributions instead of the sheriff's officers doing so. These privileges and exemptions were highly prized.

The men of Gravesend in 1401 received confirmation from Henry IV of their monopoly, already enjoyed for 200 years, of the 'long ferry' from that town to London. The right of monopoly carried with it the duty to convey passengers at a fixed rate of a halfpenny per passenger, and in 1292 some of the watermen who had been charging a penny were called upon to answer for their extortion before the Judge of Assize. The watermen were difficult to control because they were not, as were most tradesmen and artificers, organised into a trade guild. The advantages of a guild were that it regulated apprenticeships, ensured proper standards of workmanship, protected its members against unfair (and sometimes any) competition, and helped them in their old age. Maidstone in the 16th century had six guilds, or companies, namely Artificers, Cordwainers, Drapers, Haberdashers, Mercers and Victuallers, whilst Gravesend had only two, Mercers and Victuallers. By Queen Elizabeth's reign men were assigned to either company, irrespective of their occupation; trade guilds had by then become merely part of the machinery for governing the town. Earlier than the trade guilds were the merchant guilds, such as those established at Canterbury and Rochester, which gave their members valuable privileges in the local market and made it difficult for 'foreigners', as those who were not freemen of the town were called, to compete with them.

The earlier royal charters did not define the way in which the government of the town should be carried on. That was left for the burgesses to settle for themselves. However, in the 15th and 16th centuries some towns found it desirable to obtain a charter from the Crown prescribing the manner in which the town should be governed. Canterbury, for example, was granted such a charter by Henry VI in 1448. Until about the year 1200 the chief magistrate of Canterbury was known as the portreeve, and then for nearly 250 years the office was held jointly by two 'bailiffs'. For some reason not now known, the citizens decided about 1446 or 1447 that they would prefer a single 'mayor', and it was thought proper that the change should be made by royal charter. Tenterden also received a charter from Henry VI, and a few years later Edward IV granted Rochester a charter conferring on the chief magistrate the title of mayor, instead of bailiff.

The borough of Queenborough is of quite different origin from the others. As part of the defence of England at the time of his French Wars Edward III rebuilt the castle of Sheppey, and bestowed upon the castle and the surrounding district the title of Queenborough, in honour of his queen, Philippa, and gave it the status of a free borough. By the 17th century the castle was ruinous and obsolete as a defence work, so it was demolished.

Faversham possesses a fine series of no fewer than 14 charters granted by the Crown between 1252 and 1547. It was not a 'free' borough, but was in the lordship of the abbot of Faversham. Disputes between the abbot and the burgesses about their respective rights were frequent. At the time of Henry III the abbot chose the mayor annually from three men presented to him by the townsmen, but afterwards they obtained the privilege of submitting only one person to be sworn by the abbot into the office of mayor. In 1546, after the abbey had been dissolved, Henry VIII granted the town a charter providing for the government to be in the hands of a mayor, 12 jurats, and 44 freemen.

Maidstone's first charter was granted by Edward VI in 1548. The reason for the grant of the charter is explained in the preamble: for many years past the

71 *The Six Poor Travellers, Rochester*

72 *The old town pump and the corner pillar of the Guildhall in Faversham*

government of the town had been thought to belong to certain inhabitants called the portreeve and brethren, but recently the legality of the arrangement had been brought into question and it was necessary for a royal charter to be granted in order to put the government of the town on a lawful basis. Accordingly the king ordained that the town should have a mayor, to be elected every year, and a body of 13 jurats, holding office for life, who should have the same powers of government as the mayor and jurats at Canterbury. Because of the part which the inhabitants of Maidstone took in Wyatt's rebellion of 1554 Queen Mary deprived the town of its charter, but five years later Queen Elizabeth made a grant of a new charter, with wider powers. The mayor was now given the status of a justice of the peace; the inhabitants were to be exempt from jury-service outside the town; and they were empowered to elect two Members of Parliament. They also were authorised to hold a weekly market and a fair four times a year, with a Court of Piepowder (that is a court to settle summarily disputes arising at a market or fair) and to establish a grammar school.

Another town to which a charter was granted by Queen Elizabeth was Gravesend—strictly, Gravesend and Milton. Difficulties had arisen because the confirmation of the long ferry monopoly by Henry IV was to 'the men of Gravesend'. But who, exactly, were 'the men of Gravesend' possessing this right, and who was to bring a legal action if the monopoly was infringed? It was difficulties of this sort that led the medieval lawyers to hit upon the device of 'incorporation', that is the treating of a group of persons, such as the Dean and Chapter of a Cathedral, the Fellows of a College, or the mayor, jurats and commonalty of a town, as a single legal person able to bring and to defend legal proceedings and able to own land in perpetuity. Normally, a group of persons could acquire a corporate existence of this sort only by royal grant. By Queen Elizabeth's charter of 1562 the inhabitants of Gravesend were made a corporation, to be governed by two portreeves and 10 jurats. An alteration was made by a new charter granted in 1568 which recited that inconveniences had arisen from there being two portreeves (it is not difficult to guess the kind of differences that might have arisen between them), and ordained that for the future the town should be governed by a portreeve, to be chosen annually, 12 jurats, and 24 'Capital Inhabitants', who should together constitute the Common Council. The charter included the usual grants of market, fair, municipal court and power to tax the inhabitants. The monopoly of the long ferry to London was confirmed on payment of 5s. a year to the Crown. The ferry remained for centuries an important part of the town's business. The barges, which held forty or more passengers and with luck made the journey in one tide, that is five or six hours, were apparently Corporation property, the various inhabitants who had the right taking it in turn to sail (or row, if the wind failed) the barge to or from London.

The Common Council in 1595 laid down a number of regulations about the ferry; the fare was not to be more than 2d. a passenger, but unless the passengers were prepared to make up the total fare to 4s. the master of the boat was not obliged to sail; the crew was to consist of a steersman and at least four rowers, or five in foul weather; and an attempt was made to protect the barge-traffic against competition from the private enterprise ventures of smaller vessels known as tiltboats, lighthorsemen and wherries. The regulations also required a proper scheme of apprenticeship to be adopted, referring to the number of drownings that had happened in consequence of barge-masters employing 'boys and others of small skill and evil nurture'. Perhaps it was the character of the local boys that had caused the Corporation, at least as early as 1580, to establish a school wherein the master was required to teach 'his scollers manners and hollsome learning according to the lawes of this Realme'.

The oldest schools in Kent are the King's School at Canterbury, and King's School, Rochester. Each was associated with the adjacent cathedral and as to their dates of foundation perhaps it is safest to say that both had already had a long (though possibly not continuous) history by the time that the corporations of Maidstone and Gravesend established their schools during the reign of Queen Elizabeth. Sevenoaks School was founded in 1432 by Sir William Sennocke, Lord Mayor of London, for the free instruction of poor children. At Tenterden a free grammar school must already have been in existence by 1521 because in that year a gift was made to it. In a 'Free Grammar School' it was only instruction in Latin and Greek that was free; if the scholars required to be taught other subjects such as English, writing or arithmetic, they had to pay a fee to the master. It was a rule of the school which Sir Andrew Judd (another Lord Mayor of London) founded at Tonbridge in 1553 that the pupils before admission should be able to write competently, and to read perfectly, both English and Latin.

73 *Norman staircase, King's School, Canterbury*

The increasing prosperity of the county resulted in the establishment of several new schools during the Elizabethan period. Simon Lynch founded a 'free and perpetual grammar school' at Cranbrook, Sir Roger Manwood, a notable lawyer and Chief Baron of the Exchequer, gave extensive lands to Sandwich Corporation to endow a grammar school in his native town, and William Lambe, clothworker, established a similar school at Sutton Valence. The Queen herself, out of the lands which accrued to the Crown on the dissolution of Faversham Abbey, endowed a school 'for the education of the youth inhabiting there'. An earlier school had existed in the town, associated with the abbey. The Elizabethan school building, which stands a little to the north of the church, was built in 1587 and remained in use as a school for nearly three hundred years.

There were a good many more school foundations during the 17th century, of which the most important were Edward Gibbon's at Benenden in 1602; John Southlands' at New Romney in 1610; Sir Norton Knatchbull's Grammar School at Ashford in 1636/7 (the original building of which still stands in the churchyard); Launcelot Bathurst's at Staplehurst in 1639, for teaching 'poor children reading, writing and their duty towards God and man'; William Cleave's at Yalding in 1665, for teaching 'English, Writing, Accounts and the Catechism';

74 *Tonbridge School*

John Horsemonden's Free Grammar School at Goudhurst in 1670, for the teaching of Greek and Latin 'and so many of the tongues, arts and sciences as the pupils should be willing to learn'; Sir Eliab Harvey's school at Folkestone in 1674, for the teaching of 'writing and reading and (if they wish it) Latin' (these pious founders seem to have had a touching faith in the pupils' desire for learning); Lady Boswell's at Sevenoaks in 1675, for 15 poor children to be taught 'reading, writing, casting accounts and the Church catechism'; and, to extend the century by one year, Sir Joseph Williamson's School at Rochester, in 1701, for instruction in 'mathe-matics and all other things which might fit and encourage [the pupils] to the sea-service, or arts and callings leading or relating thereto'.

These various schools were by no means all of equal size and importance. The same is true of the towns themselves. Only eight of them, for example, sent representatives to Parliament: Canterbury ard Rochester; the Cinque Ports (Dover, Sandwich, Hythe and New Romney); Queenborough which was enfranchised in 1571, when it possessed only 23 inhabited houses; and Maidstone which was granted the right to return members to Parliament by Queen Elizabeth's charter of 1559. The enfranchisement of Maidstone and Queenborough was probably intended less as a benefit to the towns themselves than as a help to the Queen in achieving an agreeable House of Commons. The county itself was represented by two Knights of the Shire, who usually carried more influence in the House than the borough representatives.

Finally as a very approximate indication of the relative wealth of the towns of Kent in the earlier part of the 17th century, here are their assessments to Ship-money in 1636, when the total burden laid on the county was £8,000:

Canterbury	300
Dover, Folkestone, Faversham, Margate, St Peter's, Birchington, Kingsdown, Ringwould, etc.	330
Sandwich, Deal, Walmer, Ramsgate, Fordwich, Sarre, etc.	250
Cranbrook	200
New Romney, Lydd, Old Romney, Dengemarsh, Broomhill, etc.	180
Maidstone	160
Tenterden	90
Rochester	80
Gravesend	40
Hythe	40
Queenborough	10

The most surprising item in this list is the comparatively heavy assessment of Cranbrook; the reason for it, already hinted at, will appear more fully in the next chapter.

11

Industries in the 15th to 18th Centuries

Today, industry is almost always associated with towns. Everyone thinks of places such as Birmingham, Leeds, Manchester and Bradford, or in Kent, Erith, Dartford, Chatham and Sittingbourne as centres of industry, whatever other characteristics they may possess in addition. However, in Tudor, Elizabethan and Stuart Kent, industries were not concentrated in the towns, but were scattered over the greater part of the county. In the main, they grew up where the raw materials were to hand. The roads were so bad that the transport of heavy and bulky materials was extremely difficult and costly, and Kent is not well served by navigable rivers. Cloth-making therefore established itself near to the source of its raw material, wool and the great iron industry of the Weald grew up there because both the ore and the fuel for smelting it were readily obtainable.

The pattern of the distribution of industry did not, however, depend solely upon the ready availability of necessary raw materials. On many occasions in the 16th and 17th centuries groups of refugees fled to England in order to escape religious persecution on the Continent, and almost always they brought some industrial skill or technical knowledge with them. Thus, for example, silk-weaving came to Canterbury and market-gardening to Sandwich with the Walloon refugees about 1560-70.

The number of refugees who made their homes in England between the 1560s and the 1580s, and who, by their skill and industry, contributed valuably to the country's wealth and well-being, was certainly well over 100,000. Of these the majority settled in East Anglia, in London and in Kent. No precise population statistics are available before the first official census in 1801, when the figure given for Kent was just over 300,000. Two hundred years before, at the end of Queen Elizabeth's reign, it was probably about 150,000, of whom the 'strangers' numbered a few thousand.

Most of the people in Elizabeth's time derived their livelihood, directly or indirectly, from agriculture, which long remained the most important industry. Fruit-growing was on the increase, and hops were introduced during the 16th century, but on the whole Kent remained a county of mixed farming, with no very revolutionary changes. There was greater development of agriculture in the 18th century, and we shall therefore return to it in a later chapter.

The market-gardening industry was introduced into England by the Walloon immigrants who settled at Sandwich towards the end of the 16th century. At

75 *The Dutch House, Sandwich*

that time Englishmen were not much given to eating vegetables, and such as were required were largely imported from the Low Countries. Naturally the immigrant 'Dutchmen', as they were usually called, finding the soil and the climate suitable, re-established their market-gardening industry where they first settled. Cabbages, carrots and celery were their speciality, and even as late as 1768 Sandwich carrots were still 'esteemed the sweetest as they are the largest of any in England'. London was naturally the main market for vegetables, and within a few years some of the Walloons moved off to the outskirts of the capital, to establish market-gardens in north-west Kent and in Surrey with the advantage of a shorter journey to market. Not all of the Walloons, by any means, left Sandwich. Many remained there as flourishing market-gardeners, and from the fact that the flat land on either side of the road from Sandwich to Canterbury has the Dutch name of The Poulders (a word still in use in Holland for the parts of the Zuider Zee which have been reclaimed) suggests that the immigrant strangers used their skill in the building of walls and dykes to reclaim some of the marshland at Sandwich.

Another industry which they brought to Sandwich was the making of cloths called 'says and bays'. Without these new industries, Sandwich, its harbour silted up and unusable, would have been a dying town. How much the new industries meant to the town is shown by the fact that at the end of the 16th century the foreign immigrants, who practised the new industries, outnumbered the English inhabitants, many of whom had lost their livelihood.

Other refugees settled at Canterbury. Cloth-making had been established there for some time, for at the Dissolution the Franciscan house, the Greyfriars, became a cloth-factory. The Walloons who settled at Canterbury specialised in the making of silks, and the city soon became, with London, one of the two centres of the craft in England. This was not a case of an industry being set up near the source of its raw material, because the raw silk had to be imported from Italy and Turkey; the important 'raw material' here was the skill of the weavers. As elsewhere in the county, the refugees were generally welcomed by the authorities, for it was realised that their knowledge and industry brought prosperity to the places where they settled. At Canterbury the Huguenots, as they were called, were granted the use of a chapel in the crypt of the Cathedral so that they could continue their own religious services. They became loyal citizens, giving no trouble to the authorities, but to some extent 'keeping themselves to themselves'. For example, they looked after their own aged and poor, and therefore demurred at paying the City poor rate, although their objection to doing so was overruled by the Judge of Assize. They, and the silk-weaving industry, thrived to such an evtent that, in 1660, over 2,000 people were employed in the industry, of whom 1,300 were 'strangers' and 700 English. After the Revocation of the Edict of Nantes in 1685 more French Protestants fled to England, some of whom settled at Canterbury. The last few years of the 17th century saw the industry at its zenith. Celia Fiennes, who was a great traveller and kept a diary of all that she saw, remarked on the prosperity of the silk-weavers when she visited Canterbury in 1697: 'I saw 20 Loomes in one house with severall fine flower'd silks', she records. But, in truth, the industry was about to collapse. The opening

76 *The old Weavers' house in Canterbury*

up of trade with the East by the East India Company and the importation of woven silks was a serious blow to the silk-weavers of London and Canterbury. The attempts which were made, by Act of Parliament, to protect the home industry by restricting the importation of silk cloth were not successful and by 1710 the number of master-weavers at Canterbury had fallen by more than half. A few years later the industry was practically dead.

More than two hundred years before the first refugees arrived at Sandwich and Canterbury, the great cloth-making industry of the Weald had prospered by the introduction of skilled foreign workmen, invited over to England by Edward III, particularly from the Netherlands. Even before Edward III's time cloth-making was widespread, almost each town and village making the cloth for its own needs. There are, for example, references to the weaving of cloth at Eynsford, Dartford, Strood, Rochester, Maidstone and several places in Larkfield Hundred, Milton Regis, Canterbury and Cranbrook in the 13th century. However, cloth-making on this scale could scarcely be termed an industry and fine cloth had either to be imported from the Continent, or the coarse English cloth sent there to be finished. Edward I, during a dispute with Flanders, forbade the export of English wool or the import of Flemish cloth. It was with the same object, of strengthening the English cloth industry and weakening the rival industry in Flanders, that Edward III issued his invitation to foreign workmen to leave their homes and to settle in England. It can readily be understood that, at first, the foreigners were not everywhere well received.

One of the areas in which they settled was the Weald around Cranbrook. There was plenty of wool to be had from the Kentish flocks, although it had the reputation of being of inferior quality to the wool of East Anglia and the West Country. Moreover, two other commodities were available for finishing the cloth—water-power and fuller's earth. To cleanse it from grease the cloth had to be pounded in water and treated with fuller's earth. The pounding could be done by men treading, or walking, on the cloth in a trough, but it could be done more economically by a fulling mill in which a series of hammers were driven by water-power. The streams in the Cranbrook district could easily be dammed back to give a sufficient force of water to work mills, and at one time as many as 15 or 18 mills were at work in or near Cranbrook. The fuller's earth came from the neighbourhood of Maidstone, especially from Boxley parish.

The industry spread to other nearby villages, notably Benenden, Biddenden, Staplehurst and Tenterden and, to a less extent, Hawkhurst, Goudhurst, Horsmonden, Brenchley, Frittenden, Pluckley, Smarden, Hunton, Yalding, Leeds, Seal, Tudeley and Tonbridge. Apart from the actual weaving and fulling, many of the processes, such as spinning and carding, were carried out in the workpeople's own homes. The factory system in industry came much later, in the 18th century. The weaving was done in the master cloth-worker's 'hall' and there the raw materials and the finished products were stored. Several of these fine timber-framed cloth-workers' halls still exist, one of the best known being that at Biddenden.

77 *The Old Cloth Hall, Biddenden*

78 *All Saints Church, Biddenden. The church was much developed when the village was a prosperous local centre for the cloth workers*

Because cloth-making was carried on in small isolated units in this way, the industry had to be controlled, in the interests of the purchaser. The regulation width of Kentish broadcloth, as it was called, was 58 inches, and each piece had to be between 30 and 34 yards in length and to weigh 66 lb. Officials, known as ulnagers (from *aulne*, an ell) were appointed to see that the regulations were obeyed. No piece of cloth might be sold until it had been passed by them and sealed; offenders, principally those whose cloth was below the regulation weight, were fined. Woad, madder and saffron were amongst the materials used to dye the cloths, the principal colours being russet, ginger, orange, blue, grey and green. Eventually the Kent clothiers specialised in a grey cloth, which became so characteristic of the industry in the county that it was known as Kentish grey.

So many processes were involved in cloth-making that the manufacture of a single piece required the labour of 30 to 40 men, women and children. Most of the clothiers worked on a fairly small scale although a few carried on business in a larger way—Thomas Davy of Cranbrook, for example, was authorised in 1519 to export 1,000 unfinished cloths within the next seven years, and when Robert Hovenden, of Frizley in Cranbrook, died in 1615 he had on hand finished cloths and raw materials worth nearly £450, so both Davy and Hovenden must have been manufacturers of some account. So also was James Skeate of Tenterden who sent to London 40 or 50 cloths a year. The

79 *Cranbrook Mill*

value of Kentish broadcloth at this time was about £12 to £16 a piece, that is about 8s. to 11s. a yard.*

It was estimated, during Queen Elizabeth's reign, that the output of cloth in the Weald amounted to 11,000 or 12,000 pieces a year, so the total value must have been about £150,000, a very large sum of money for those days.

The clothiers constantly believed that the industry was in a precarious state, and sought to have it protected against foreign competition by Act of Parliament. Towards the end of the 17th century trade was beginning to fall away seriously, and by the end of the next century the great cloth-making industry of the Weald was at an end. It was not so much foreign competition, as competition from the growing and more favourably situated cloth manufactories of Yorkshire, Somerset, Wiltshire and Gloucester, that caused the collapse of the industry in Kent.

At the height of its prosperity, about 1580, Cranbrook supported a population of some 3,000, at a time when Maidstone's population was not more than about 2,000. Maidstone owes much of its importance to its situation at the point where the road from London and Sevenoaks to Ashford and the coast crosses the Medway. However, in the 16th and 17th centuries this road carried much less traffic than Watling Street and it was not until the latter half of the 19th century that Maidstone surpassed Rochester, Chatham and Canterbury in size. For its development in the 17th century Maidstone had to thank four local industries—the making of cloths called 'mannikins', the export of fuller's earth from Boxley, the dressing of linen, and the making of linen-thread. The latter was another of the industries introduced by Flemish refugees at the end of the 16th century. During the following century it flourished to such an extent that it was said that Maidstone thread was 'carried all over the world', but in 1668 the thread-makers of Maidstone were petitioning Parliament to protect their industry from unfair competition and especially from the import of Dutch thread. The industry survived into, but not until the end of, the 18th century.

We must now return to the Weald. The clothiers of the Cranbrook district complained in 1635 that the prosperity of their industry was threatened by the setting up of John Browne's ironworks, which consumed vast quantities of timber. The iron-ore of the Weald had been worked and smelted as early as Roman times, but more on the Sussex than the Kent side of the forest. The smelting of ore was certainly being carried on at Tudeley as early as the beginning of the 14th century, and at the end of the 16th century there were

*The wages of a farm-worker would be about 3s. 6d. a week, of a skilled artisan perhaps twice that figure.

IX *Dover Castle, one of the finest medieval castles surviving. In the foreground is the Palace Gate. Note the top of the great late 12th-century keep, and the inner bailey walls of the same period.*

X *Folkestone after a rain storm. In the foreground is part of the harbour, and the brick arches of the railway connecting the jetty with the main line system. In the distance is a section of the Downs, which tumble into the sea at this part of the coast.*

XI *Rochester. The view from the top of the old keep built to guard the crossing. The bridge seen here over the river Medway is the latest of many built to carry the Kentish section of the great Roman road of Watling Street between the Channel ports and London.*

XII *The beautiful Bagham Mill on the banks of the river Stour near Chilham. It is now the property of the water company and is being completely restored to its full working condition.*

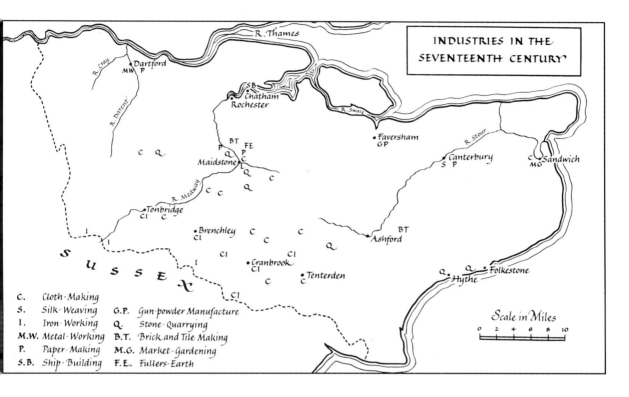

80 *Map showing the location of industries in the 17th century*

ironworks at Cranbrook, Hawkhurst, Goudhurst, Horsmonden, Tonbridge, Cowden, Ashurst, Brenchley, Lamberhurst and Biddenden.

Iron-making involved two processes: first the smelting of the ore in a 'bloomery', and then the refining of the metal so produced. A bloomery consisted of a kiln, in shape rather like the old lime-kilns which are still to be seen in various parts of the county, about 24 ft. in diameter and 30 ft. high, open at the top. The ore and the fuel (wood and charcoal) were fed in from the top in alternate layers and the furnace was then set burning. To get the necessary temperature a good draught was required. Bellows were therefore installed, being worked either by a couple of men or by water-power. The metal collected in a molten mass at the bottom of the furnace and was drawn off into a depression in the ground. Then it had to be reheated and beaten to get rid of impurities. It was found that water-power could be used for working the hammers in the same way as it was used for working the fulling-mills, and contemporary travellers in the Weald speak of the hideous noise which the hammer-furnaces made. Nothing of them now remains, but their situation is often indicated by names such as Hammer Pond, Hammer Stream, Furnace Pond, Cinderhill Wood, Cinder Lane and Blower's Cottage. The iron was used for making horseshoes and nails, for which the demand was enormous; pots, pans, firebacks, hinges and so on; and cannon-balls and cannon. Casting cannon was a highly skilled business, and Kentish cannon were not only used in royal castles and ships, but were also exported, sometimes lawfully and sometimes smuggled out of the country under loads of brushwood.

Browne's ironworks at Brenchley, one of the largest, was employing 200 men in the early part of the 17th century. The consumption of timber for fuel was enormous: one works alone was said to burn 750,000 cubic feet in a single year. The Weald was still heavily wooded, but the exhaustion of the timber supply was a constant source of anxiety to the people of Kent, and to the government. The scarcity of timber, the importation of iron from Sweden, Flanders and Spain, and the discovery that coal (which was not to be had in the Weald) could be used for smelting iron-ore, caused the decline of the Kentish iron industry from about the 1660s until by 1740 only four furnaces were still at work in the county.

Some of the iron made in the Weald no doubt found its way to Dartford where, in 1590, Godfrey Box, an immigrant from Liège, set up the first slitting-mill in England for cutting iron bars into rods. About the same time another mill was established at Crayford for the manufacture of iron plates for armour. The engineering industry at Dartford and Crayford can, therefore, claim a long ancestry.

Dartford was also a pioneer town in paper-making. The mill which Spielman, a German, set up there early in the reign of Elizabeth was the second paper-mill to be opened in England. The Darent provided the power to drive the mill, and also the supply of clean water that is essential for paper-making. Spielman was given a monopoly of the making of white paper for 10 years and was authorised to 'gather all manner of linen rags ... scraps of parchment, leather shreds, clippings of cards, and old fishing nets, necessary for the making of ... white writing-paper'. He employed no fewer than 600 men, many of them, like himself, Germans. In the 18th century the mill was purchased by Pigou and Wilks, who used it for the manufacture of gunpowder. The paper-making industry in Kent received a big impetus from the arrival of refugee Frenchmen after the Revocation of the Edict of Nantes (1685) and many French terms are still employed in the industry; the large room where the paper is finished, for example, is still called the *salle*. By the end of the 17th century there were several mills at work in Kent, including a second mill at Dartford, a brown-paper mill at Canterbury, and a very small mill at Aylesford within a few hundred yards of the enormous mill built by Messrs. Albert E. Reed & Co. Ltd in the 1920s and 1930s. Quite possibly this little mill at Aylesford had been converted from a corn-mill, in the same way as a fulling-mill at Boxley, the Old Turkey Mill, was converted into a paper-mill by James Whatman in 1739 and produced paper which was of such quality that the words 'Whatman' and 'Turkey Mill' are now trade-names for first-class hand-made papers. Other mills were built at Maidstone and Tovil in the 18th century, the Len and the Loose Valley stream being the source of water and of power.

Gunpowder, as already mentioned, was made at Dartford in the 18th century. It had also been manufactured at Faversham, on a larger scale, from Elizabethan times. The Faversham mills flourished during the 18th and 19th centuries (apart from a disastrous explosion or two) and did not close down

81 *Ship building on the beach*

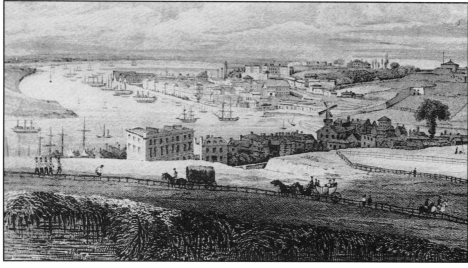

82 *Chatham from the hill by Fort Pitt*

until the beginning of this century. The stream which runs down through Ospringe into Faversham Creek provided the power to drive the mills.

Faversham Creek is now the site of a boat-building yard, and probably the industry has been carried on there in a small way for centuries. It was carried on in a much larger way at the royal dockyards, at Deptford, Woolwich and Chatham. Deptford was in use as a shipbuilding yard at least by the year 1400 but Woolwich and Chatham did not follow until the 16th century. All three of the yards derived much of their timber, especially oak, for the building and repair of ships from the Weald. Its transport presented great difficulty because

83 *Weather-boarded houses, Gravesend*

the roads were unbelievably bad, often being totally impassable after prolonged rain.

Oak and Spanish chestnut were also largely used for the building of houses in the Weald and on those parts of the North Downs where the clay overlying the chalk carried timber-forest. The timber-framed house, the space between the timbers being filled in with plaster, is still typical of the Weald. In the 18th century fir-planks began to be imported from the Baltic and were used for the construction of those weather-boarded cottages and houses which are as characteristic of 18th-century building in the Weald as timber-framed construction was typical of the 15th and 16th centuries.

Stone, of a kind which in the Middle Ages was used for church-, castle- and house-building, had been worked in Kent from Roman times. The great ragstone quarries at Maidstone, Boughton Monchelsea, Loose, Tovil, Offham and Allington; at Folkestone, Hythe and Sandgate; and at Ightham, for many centuries provided an excellent building material, used for buildings as far apart in time as St Leonard's Tower, West Malling (*c.*1100) and Preston Hall, Aylesford (*c.*1850). The ragstone was not only used for building but also for cannon-balls, at least up to the time of Henry VIII. Around Bethersden a particularly fine limestone known as Bethersden marble was quarried from medieval times onwards, and was used locally for building, and in more distant parts of the county for ornamental features, such as columns and tombs. In the south-west corner of the county the sandstone found around Tunbridge Wells has been extensively used for building, as, for example, at Penshurst Place. At the other end of the county, in Thanet, and around Dover and Deal, the chalk contains bands of flint which was mined and often used in church- and in house-building until the end of the 19th century.

At many places in the county the clay or brick-earth is suitable for the manufacture of tiles and bricks and has been so used for centuries. Battle Abbey, which owned the great manor of Wye, had a tile-works at Naccolt with an annual output of more than 100,000 tiles, at least as early as 1340. Similarly, in the 14th century, the monks of Boxley had their own tile-yards, and in the following century we hear of a large brick-ground belonging to the Corporation of Sandwich. From that time onwards bricks and tiles were increasingly in demand, and although some were imported through Kentish ports from the Netherlands and Flanders, the industry expanded rapidly in Kent, especially as the rebuilding of London after the Fire of 1666 and its expansion during the 18th century offered a profitable market for the produce of Kent brickfields.

It is to this variety of local building materials that Kent owes the pleasing variety of its architecture.

The quarrying of stone is an 'extractive' industry; so also, although of a very different kind, is the industry formerly pursued by all the Kentish ports from Gravesend round to New Romney, namely the extraction of fish from the sea. Before the Dissolution, the religious houses had consumed vast quantities of fish, and there was always a ready market for it. There were famous oyster-fisheries at Reculver, Whitstable, Faversham, Milton Regis and in the mouth of the Medway. So valuable were they that from time to time they were raided by men from Essex and by Dutchmen. Elsewhere around the coast a whole variety of fish were caught. Daniel Rough, the Town Clerk of Romney, wrote out a list about 1350 of the taxes which were payable on goods bought or sold in the town, and it includes cod, porpoise, herring and sprats; elsewhere he refers also to crabs, salmon, haddock, lampreys, mackerel, conger, shrimps, whiting, tench and eels. So long as the main fishing grounds were near the coast, or at least not farther off than the Dogger Bank, the Kent fishing industry remained prosperous, and in the 18th century the Broadstairs fishermen were even going as far afield as the cod fisheries of Iceland. Indeed, the Kent fishermen on many occasions showed enterprise in going off to new grounds, and it is only during the last few years that the industry has finally declined to a fraction of what it was a hundred years ago.

This chapter has dealt, in the main, with Kentish industries from 1500 to 1700, but it has inevitably overstepped its temporal bounds in both directions. We must resume a more strictly chronological approach, and return to the 16th century.

12

The Defence of Tudor and Stuart Kent

The Reformation not only set the king at the head of the Church of England, and brought about the dissolution of the monasteries; it also nearly involved England in a war with Catholic Europe. In 1535 Henry VIII declared himself to be the Supreme Head on Earth of the Church, a declaration which was answered by the Bull of Excommunication drawn up by the Pope in August of the same year. The Pope gave authority for another Bull to be prepared, depriving Henry VIII of his kingdom, but as the two great Catholic powers, France and the Empire, were then in a state of enmity, no effective action could be taken against England and the king remained quietly in possession of his crown.

Three years later the position had changed. France and the Empire were drawing together, and at the end of 1538 the Pope ordered the Bull of Excommunication to be put into force. The danger of invasion now became serious and the government began to strengthen the coastal defences. At Gravesend, and at the adjacent town of Milton, two forts were constructed, armed with cannon; and two similar forts were built at Tilbury on the other side of the Thames. Thus were London and its river approaches protected. The urgency with which these fortifications were run up is shown by the fact that, at Gravesend, there was no time to buy the land on which the blockhouses were built, and it was not acquired by the Crown until three years later. At Queenborough the castle built by Edward III nearly two hundred years earlier was put into repair. On the Channel coast bulwarks, mounting cannon were built at Dover, but the most vulnerable point was thought to be the flat shore around Deal, the shore on which Julius Caesar landed in 55 and 54 B.C. To guard it, three castles were built; at Sandown, just to the north of Deal, at Deal itself and at Walmer. Sandown Castle has been destroyed but the other two remain, Walmer Castle being the official residence of the Lord Warden of the Cinque Ports. Farther to the south another fort was built at Sandgate, and across the Marsh, just over the Sussex border, the last in the series of Henry VIII's Channel castles was erected at Camber.

Camber Castle was largely demolished in the 17th century for the sake of the materials, and Sandgate Castle, altered a good deal at the time of the Napoleonic War, has been seriously damaged by the sea. Deal and Walmer are the only two that remain, and they have been considerably altered from their original form, although at Deal a well-aimed bomb during the 1939-45 war

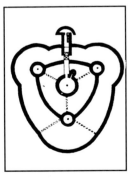

84 *Plan of Sandgate Castle*

85 *Walmer Castle*

neatly removed some of the later additions. The castles were roughly circular in plan, about 300 ft. in diameter overall, and with a central tower, or keep, which mounted cannon with a wide arc of fire. Sandown Castle was guarded by a captain and 34 men, and no doubt the garrisons of the others were about the same size. The complete accounts for the building of Sandgate Castle are now at the British Museum. They show that, from start to finish, the building of the castle took 18 months and cost £2,887 14s. Work had to be suspended because of frost during the winter months, and in any case there was a three weeks' holiday at Christmas. Bad weather caused the loss of something like three months, so the actual building time was only 15 months. The government clearly regarded it as an urgent work and the master-mason of the King's Palace of Hampton Court was put in charge. During one month no fewer than 900 men were engaged, either directly on building operations or on carting stone and timber, and at several other times there were upwards of 500 men on the pay-roll. Much of the stone was quarried locally within a mile of the castle, but some came second-hand from the recently dismantled priories at St Radegund's, Monks Horton and Christ Church, Canterbury.

To build castles was not enough; men, too, were needed, and in March 1539, the government ordered the forces of Kent to be mustered to resist the expected invasion. Each Hundred sent its men, but the total fell short of the county's quota, and many of those who came were ill-equipped and poorly trained. It was fortunate that, after all, the feared invasion was not attempted.

It was a combination of religious differences and foreign affairs that gave rise to the next disturbance in Kent, Wyatt's rebellion in January 1554. Queen Mary, who succeeded to the throne in 1553, restored the Catholic religion, and

betrothed herself to Philip, the Catholic King of Spain. The betrothal was unpopular in England and there were risings in several parts of the country. Of these the most serious was that in Kent. Sir Thomas Wyatt, the son of the poet of the same name, lived at Allington Castle near Maidstone, and could perhaps best be described as a gentleman-adventurer with rather more of the adventurer than the gentleman about him. He had a direct personal interest in the preservation of the Reformation because he had acquired the property of the dissolved Friary at Aylesford. On 25 January Wyatt issued his proclamation at Maidstone, Ashford and Milton Regis, and on the 26th at Tonbridge. He set up his camp at Rochester and within a few days had collected 4,000 followers. The men of Tonbridge were put to flight in a skirmish with Lord Abergavenny's forces at Blacksole Field, Wrotham, but they managed to join the main body at Rochester. A force of 600 Londoners which was sent to Strood to intercept Wyatt at once deserted to him. Wyatt then began to advance towards London. On 30 January he captured Cooling Castle which was defended, not very stoutly perhaps, by Lord Cobham, and later the same day he was at Gravesend. On 31 January Wyatt reached Dartford. Unwisely he then loitered for two days at Greenwich and Deptford, and when he got to Southwark late on 3 February he found the gates closed on London Bridge and the city prepared to defend itself against him. A few days later he made his way to the city by way of Kingston, but he found no support in London and after a little fighting he surrendered. A few months later his life came to an end on the scaffold.

So long as Mary and her Spanish husband were on the throne there was no danger of foreign invasion but the danger revived when Protestant Elizabeth succeeded Catholic Mary in 1558. In 1559 war with France was expected, and although the peace was preserved for that year, the threat seemed merely postponed, not removed. Defensive measures were set on foot, especially in the mouth of the Medway. From 1547 onwards the reach of the river off Gillingham was increasingly important as an anchorage for the navy, and storehouses were rented on the Chatham bank of the river. To protect both ships and storehouses a castle was built on the opposite bank of the river, at Upnor, in 1560-2. A few years later the river was further defended by a great chain of iron which could be stretched across from the castle to the opposite bank and thus prevent the passage of hostile ships.

As the danger from France receded, so the danger of a Spanish invasion increased. The queen's government was constantly issuing orders for the training of the county militia. A certificate of 1580 gives the number of footmen who ought to turn out. Excluding the cities of Canterbury and Rochester, for which no figures were given, the total number was 14,217, consisting of pikemen, gunners, archers, billmen, pioneers, carpenters, smiths, masons and wheelwrights. The separate figures for the Cinque Ports, which are included in the total of 14,217, are worth quoting because they roughly indicate the relative sizes of the ports at that time: Dover, 352; Sandwich, 409; Folkestone, 135; New Romney, 128; Lydd, 239; Tenterden, 248; Faversham, 20; St John's (Margate), St Peter's (Broadstairs) and Birchington, 374. There were, in addition, a much smaller number of horsemen. It is unlikely that more than perhaps half of the total number of men ever turned out at the same muster.

One serious problem which faced the government was how, in an emergency, to get the news of a threatened landing to London quickly, and then to issue orders for the militia to be called out. The first problem was met by putting into working order the system of warning-beacons which was already at least two centuries old. Watchers were placed at high points along the coast, and if they saw a hostile fleet approaching, they set fire to their warning beacon. The watchers inland gave the warning to others on the route to London. Thus, in a few hours, news of the enemy's approach would reach the government.

The beacons were originally simply bonfires on the ground. Later iron baskets were erected on poles, and the fire was made of pitch, so that it would blaze up quickly. Frequently instructions were sent down to Kent that the beacons were to be manned. Then each beacon had to be attended day and night without break by two men, watching for the distant light that betokened the enemy, and ready at a moment to relay the warning by setting fire to their own beacon. The men worked in shifts, but it must have been a tense, yet boring, job, to stand there hour after hour whilst nothing happened. For stand they were supposed to, lest if they sat they fell asleep. Sometimes the Hundred would put up a little shed to protect the watchers from the worst of the weather, but it had to be so small that they could not sit down in it.

Lambarde, who wrote a history of Kent in 1570, the first history of any county ever written, published a map showing the beacon system in Kent (page 106). He was attacked for publishing it because it was said that he was giving useful information to the enemy, but Lambarde defended himself by arguing that the publication of the map would enable the watchers to operate the system more efficiently.

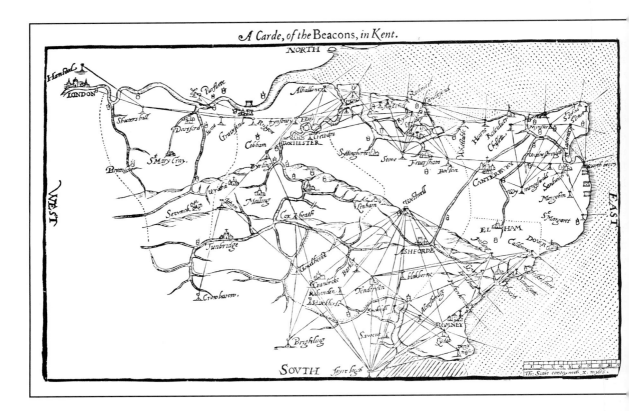

87 *William Lambarde's map showing the beacon system in Kent*

As a system, it suffered from two obvious handicaps. The first was tha unless the weather was clear the beacons could not be seen over long distances— the beacon at Fairlight, near Hastings (*Fayre leegh* on Lambarde's map), fo example, was about 18-20 miles away from Westwell. However, an invasio was unlikely to be attempted except during the summer, so the chances of mi or continuous rain were fairly remote. The other handicap was that, throug mischievousness or nervousness, a false alarm might be given. That happene on a few occasions, and the Kentishmen who mustered and prepared to resi the invasion later made it very plain to Her Majesty's Council that they wer not amused.

The great attempt to invade finally came in 1588, when the Armada saile from Spain, and came within sight of England on 15 July. It was expected tha a landing would be attempted in Kent or in Essex, since it was known that th Spaniards sailing up the Channel intended to join up with their fellow countrymen crossing from the Netherlands, then in Spanish hands. A bridge o boats was intended to be built across the Thames at Gravesend, so that me could be moved hurriedly north or south of the river as the need might deman but whether the bridge was actually finished in time is doubtful: Hakluyt cryptic phrase is 'there were certain ships brought to make a bridge, though were very late first'. The beacons presumably blazed out their warning, and th forces of the county prepared to resist the invaders. They assembled on 29 July and remained under arms until 19 August. Sir Thomas Scott, of Smeeth, was in charge of the 3,513 footmen and Sir James Hales was general of the horse, who numbered only 336—lancers 65, light horsemen 85 and carabineers 186. The wages which they received during their 22 days of service ranged from Sir Thomas Scott's and Sir James Hales' 13s. 4d. a day to the ordinary footman's 8d. a day. The number which assembled was much smaller than the number which Her Majesty's Privy Council had ordered to be levied. The Council's order spoke of 6,000 soldiers, 600 pioneers and all the companies of horse in the county. Probably the government always demanded a larger number than they knew to be possible.

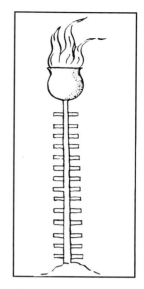

88 *A beacon, Isle of Thanet*

On the very day that the militia assembled the English and the Spanish fleets were fighting in the Strait of Dover, the only general engagement of the campaign. Better seamanship and more easily handled ships gave the English the victory, but the Spanish fleet was far from being destroyed. It sailed away into the North Sea, but the weather proved its greatest enemy. Storms arose and drove many of the Spanish ships on to the coasts of Scotland and Ireland, and the crippled Armada tried to make its way home again by circumnavigating the British Isles. Of the 30,000 sailors and soldiers who had sailed away from Spain in the Invincible Armada, fewer than half ever returned to their own country.

We now know, but the Elizabethans were not to know, that the failure of the Armada brought to an end the danger of invasion. War with Spain continued, and from time to time Kent was called upon to supply small contingents of men, as far as possible chosen from those willing to be employed for service overseas. The defences of the county were constantly being looked to, and several of the larger towns were ordered to lay in stocks of gunpowder. In May 1591, the Spanish fleet was again in the English Channel and the Privy Council ordered the beacons in Kent to be carefully watched and guarded. In September 1592, there was another similar alarm and again precautions were taken.

Three years later a landing in Kent and Essex was feared, and Kent was commanded to raise 6,000 foot soldiers, the number for the adjoining counties being: Sussex, Surrey and Essex 4,000 each, and London 3,000. Training went on during the winter, but was much hampered by the excessively wet weather. In April 1596, the Spaniards attacked Calais and Kent was ordered to send 3,000 men to Dover immediately to cross to the French coast; but 'Calais was lost before our men could come'. In June 1596, Drake with a combined English and Dutch fleet sacked Cadiz, and the government expected that the King of Spain would seek his revenge. Once again Kent was ordered to raise 3,000 men, all the inhabitants of the county having horses were to keep them ready in their stables, all spreaders of false rumours were to be committed to gaol, and the militia was to be ready instantly to go to Upnor Castle. Once more the danger did not materialise. Yet again in November 1596, a Spanish fleet was at sea and the militia was put into a state of readiness to resist an attack. However, it did not come. In August 1599, for the last time, the militia was called out, but by now Philip of Spain was dead and the danger of an invasion of England had receded into the background. The invasion alarm of

89 *Sir Thomas Scott*

90 *Upnor Castle, built beside the river Medway by Elizabeth I*

91 *One of the Queen's ships at Rochester, 1588*

1599 was, in fact, quite baseless, and the government allowed the defensive preparations quietly to fade away.

The peace-at-any price policy of the earlier Stuarts, the decline of Spain and the involvement of the continental powers in the Thirty Years War gave England half a century of respite from anxiety about defence against foreign invasion. Cromwell's vigorous foreign policy was based on the superiority of the English navy over its rivals, and it was not until Charles II's Dutch Wars that home defence again became an urgent question. In 1667 Pepys wrote in his diary: 'Everybody nowadays reflect upon Oliver and commend him: what brave things he did, and made all the neighbour princes fear him.' The occasion which prompted this comment was the raid which the Dutch fleet made on the Thames and the Medway in June 1667. Commissioner Pett, who was in charge of the Dockyard at Chatham, was 'in a very fearful stink,' wrote Pepys, 'for fear of the Dutch', and well he might be, for the defence preparations were hopelessly inadequate. Fire-ships were fitted out to attack the Dutch, but they were ineffectual. The uncompleted fort at Sheerness was destroyed by a Dutch landing party of 800 men; of the fort's 16 guns only seven were serviceable, and most of the garrison hurriedly decamped leaving one man dead and seven to be taken prisoner. Slowly the Dutch fleet made its way up the Medway, arriving at Chatham two days after taking Sheerness fort. At Chatham all was in confusion, the men at the Dockyard being much more concerned to get their personal possessions than the King's ships out of harm's way. The chain stretched across the river failed to prevent the advance of the Dutch ships. Of the 22 English warships lying in the river or drawn up on the bank, one of the largest, the *Royal Charles*, was carried off and several others were set on fire and destroyed. The Dutch behaved in a leisurely fashion, sailing about in the mouth of the Medway and in the Thames estuary for a week or two, and on one occasion landing a party on the Isle of Sheppey to collect sheep and other necessaries. Belatedly the English prepared defensive positions and a fortnight after the Dutch withdrawal 60 or 70 guns had been mounted at Chatham, and ships had been sunk in the Thames above Gravesend to obstruct the channel lest the enemy should try to attack London. From Pepys' account, these seem to have been panic measures, carried out in great confusion: 'among them that are sunk they have gone and sunk without consideration the *Franakin* one of the King's ships, with stores to a very considerable value ...; and the new ship at Bristol and much wanted there'. It was not surprising that for 20 miles around the Medway towns people fled from their homes, and the news that a peace had been arranged towards the end of July must have been joyfully received by the county of Kent.

13

The Civil War

It is ironical that the only occasion during their history when Henry VIII's castles at Deal, Walmer and Sandown were engaged in action was in the course of the Civil War. How astonished would that Tudor autocrat have been to find his defence works playing a part, albeit a minor one, in a war between a king and his insubordinate parliament!

The discontents which led up to the Civil War are part of the general history of the kingdom. One of the problems was that the business of governing the country was becoming increasingly expensive and the payment of taxes, in any form, has never been a popular activity, even where all the constitutional proprieties have been observed and parliament's consent has been obtained. The attempts of King Charles I to raise money by means which were only dubiously legal, and certainly were novel, were therefore bound to meet with opposition. In 1626 the king required his loving subjects to grant him a 'loan', Kent's share of which was fixed at £6,711 (Canterbury at £402 and Rochester at £120). Maximilian Dalison and Richard Parker were appointed to collect the money in Kent and found their task a difficult one. In truth, considering the size and wealth of the county, it was not a formidable sum; the poor escaped altogether and the well-to-do could have afforded to contribute, without hardship, the few pounds that each was called upon to lend. But they were naturally reluctant to part with their money and, besides, the principle of 'forced loans' was resented.

In 1635 the king made his first general demand for 'ship-money'. It was true that the defence of the kingdom required a larger and better equipped Royal Navy and the maritime counties were accustomed to having to find ships, or money in lieu of ships, from time to time for the king's service. It seemed no more than fair that this burden, instead of being limited to the maritime counties, should be spread over the whole country. However, the legality of imposing ship-money on the inland counties was doubtful, the money was certainly not all spent on the navy, and it became almost an annual tax. The amounts which Kent was called upon to pay were as follows:

First Assessment	October 1635	£8,000
Second Assessment	November 1636	£8,000
Third Assessment	December 1637	£8,000
Fourth Assessment	January 1639	£2,750
Fifth Assessment	February 1640	£8,000

On this last occasion the Crown offered to accept £6,400 instead of £8,000 if payment was made promptly. The fact that the king was prepared to offer a 20 per cent discount for a speedy settlement indicates the delay which was being experienced in collecting ship-money, a delay which increased with every fresh assessment. It remains only to say that the Kentishmen did not earn the 20 per cent discount and large arrears were still outstanding months after the date for payment had passed.

Ship-money was by no means the only imposition that the county suffered. In March 1639 Kent was required to find 1,000 men, out of the trained bands, who were to assemble at Gravesend and embark there for service against the Scots. This was to be done at the charge of the county, a matter of £1,500. The names of those to go were drawn out of a hat. Some who were thus selected to go managed to find others to take their places, at a cost of about £7 a man— 50s. for a new suit of clothes, 20s. to put in his purse, and £3 or so for equipment. They did not see action in the north because peace was patched up between the king and the Scots. In April of the following year Kent was required to find £1,750 to sustain the 1,000 men (700 from the county and 300 from the Cinque Ports) who were once again required to assemble at Gravesend for service in the north. But the money was slow in coming in, many of the men and their equipment were found to be unserviceable (deliberate inefficiency is hinted at) and the men were semi-mutinous.

In 1641 six of the traditional taxes called subsidies were levied between April and December, each of something like £6,000 for the whole county, but the later ones were not fully collected. In April 1642 another subsidy was levied, and the amount laid on Kent was no less than £20,281 15s. 7½d. It is improbable that the whole amount was raised.

Taxation was by no means the only cause for discontent. On Church matters the country was deeply divided, and Archbishop Laud's attempts to reform the Church on Anglo-Catholic principles caused grave offence in some quarters. In 1640 petitions were sent up to Parliament from various parts of Kent, including Canterbury and the Weald, protesting against Laud's reforms. In 1641 Sir John Colepepper presented a petition from Kent in which the grievances set out were concerned partly with taxation and partly with ecclesiastical matters, and when in May 1642 a Bill was introduced in the House of Commons to abolish episcopacy 'root and branch', its first reading was moved by Sir Edward Dering of Surrenden, one of the Knights of the Shire for Kent. At this time, therefore, it could be said that Kent, on the whole, supported Parliament rather than the Royalist cause, but the confusing series of petitions and counter-petitions which were sent up in the name of the county is an indication that opinion in Kent was far from being unanimous. However, the county had few extremists of either party and hoped generally for a moderate and reasonable settlement.

In February 1642 Sir Michael Livesey of Eastchurch organised a petition in the name of 'the Knights, Gentry and Commonalty of the County of Kent' which expressed moderate support for the reforming party. The county gentlemen who met at Maidstone for the Assizes in March took the opportunity of getting up another petition, again quite moderate in tone, which first explained that

92 *Archbishop Laud*

previous petitions had not, like the present one, come from an assembled body of the county, and then went on to make a number of reasonable requests such as that 'a good understanding be come to between King and Parliament' and that a law be framed 'for the regulating of the Militia of this Kingdom so that the subjects may know how at once to obey both His Majesty and the Houses of Parliament'. For the king and parliament had been issuing conflicting orders about the Militia and so placing in a dilemma the many law-abiding subjects, forming the vast majority, who wished to disobey neither king nor parliament. Moderate as was the petition, by no means all of the 19 gentlemen present were prepared to support it, for they knew that it would give offence to parliament; indeed, it seems to have been carried by a majority of only one vote. The intention was that signatures to the petition should be collected in various parts of the county and that it should then be carried up to Westminster. However, parliament heard about the petition from some of its supporters at Maidstone, and on 30 March Sir George Strode, Sir Edward Dering, Richard Spencer and Sir Roger Twysden, four of those who had been associated with it, were ordered by the two Houses to be arrested. Nevertheless, men continued to sign the petition, which was brought up to London on 29 April by 200 Kentish gentlemen and presented to parliament by Richard Lovelace. He was promptly committed to the Gate-house, and it was while he was incarcerated there that he wrote the charming lyric 'Stone walls do not a prison make'.

93 *Sir Roger Twysden*

In the same month Edward Blunt got up a counter-petition in support of parliament. At the July Assizes at Maidstone parliament sent a group of gentlemen to sit, without any lawful warrant, on the Bench and join with the Judge in doing justice; the true reason for their presence was to ensure that the Grand Jury did not draw up any more petitions. Parliament's action in sending a commission to over-awe the Grand Jury so incensed some of the more extreme Royalists (including Sir John Manny of Linton Place, Sir John Tufton of The Mote, Sir Edward Filmer of East Sutton, Sir Anthony St Leger of Wierton and Mr. Rycaut of the Friars, Aylesford) that they drew up a direction to Augustine Skinner, one of the two Knights of the Shire, to protest to Parliament in the name of the Commons of Kent. Skinner seems to have been too cautious and moderate a man to present the petition of Manny and his friends.

By the summer of 1642 the situation had become too serious for petitions and counter-petitions to be of any use. In August the king set up his standard at Nottingham, and the Civil War had begun. Amongst the quite small number of Kentish gentlemen who sent the king support were Lord Lovelace, the Earl of Thanet, Sir Edward Dering, Sir William Clark of Hollingbourne, Richard Thornhill of Olantigh, near Wye, and Colonel Spence of Orpington. Sir Jacob Astley of the Old Palace, Maidstone, and Sir John Colepepper of Leeds Castle, both moderate men, were members of the King's Council of War.

Three days before the king raised his standard at Nottingham parliamentarian soldiers made an expedition into Kent, visiting the houses of known Royalist sympathisers and removing not only arms and armour but also money and other goods. At Rochester the castle was taken over without resistance because the garrison were out harvesting and the captain was playing bowls. Divine

94 *Sir Jacob Astley, Major General of the King's Army*

Service in the Cathedral was interrupted by the soldiers who destroyed the altar-rails and other furniture that they considered to be ungodly. Canterbury Cathedral suffered similarly three days later, and some of the medieval window-glass there was smashed. As usually happens when violence replaces argument and reason, the extremists began to take the lead, and Sir Michael Livesey was obliged to apologise to the Dean and Chapter for the behaviour of his men.

Obviously it was of importance to parliament to secure Dover Castle, the foremost military stronghold in the county. It was captured on the night of 21 August by a dozen townsmen who scaled the walls, surprised the guard and got possession of the whole castle. The garrison consisted of only 20 men, who put up no resistance. Indeed the Governor, Sir Edward Boys, probably connived at the capture of the castle; certainly he is to be found a few months later serving on the Parliamentarian County Committee of Kent. At Deal, Walmer and Sandown Castles there was no resistance. The towns, for the most part, received the soldiers amicably, and so speedily did they go about their work that, by 3 September, they were back in London, all possibility of serious trouble in Kent removed. Several prominent Royalists were safely under lock and key, some of them in Upnor Castle. More than fifty of them suffered sequestration, that is, their estates were taken into parliament's hands and the owners recovered them only by paying a lump sum of money which, in the case of Sir William Boteler of Teston and Sir George Sondes of Throwley, exceeded £3,000. No doubt sequestration was intended, in part, as a punishment of those who adhered to the king's cause, but it was devised also as a means of raising money so that parliament could meet its military expenses.

During the early part of the Civil War conditions in Kent remained quiet. The major campaigns took place in the Midlands and the only fighting in Kent was a rising in July 1643. It began at Ightham, where the minister refused to comply with parliament's ordinance that all clergy should impose upon their parishioners the oath of assistance to the parliamentary forces. Quickly the disturbance spread to Sevenoaks where 2,000 men assembled. Sir Henry Vane, M.P., of Hadlow, was sent down by parliament to reason with them, but they would not give him a hearing. The insurgents met the parliamentary troops between Sevenoaks and Tonbridge, and apparently gave as good as they received, but the final issue could not be in doubt. Thomas Stanley, the Mayor of Maidstone, a man with moderate leanings, tried to persuade the insurgents to lay down their arms, but by now they had got out of hand. Many of them had joined only for the sake of those opportunities for plunder that every insurrection affords. Thomas Weller, who held Tonbridge Castle for parliament, overheard this conversation between two of the men who had broken into his house:

> *Parry*: We have sped well here. Let us go to Hadlow and Peckham and plunder there, for they are rich rogues, and so will we go away into the woods.
> *Smale*: But we must plunder none but Roundheads.
> *Parry*: We will make every man a Roundhead that hath anything to lose. This is the time we look for.

But within a week a parliamentary force despatched from London defeated the insurgents in a three-hour engagement at Tonbridge and brought the rising to an end. It was an affair of little real importance, unlike the rising which took place five years later, in 1648, when a large part of the county was up in arms.

That a county which, on the whole, was well disposed towards the parliamentary side and always inclined towards moderate courses should be driven within five years from a well-behaved, mannerly attitude into insurrection needs explanation. Much of the blame must be laid at the door of the County Committee by which Kent was governed. The County Committee was evolved from the Deputy Lieutenants for the county and was never formally constituted under an ordinance of parliament. There were sub-committees for each of the Lathes and separate sub-committees for Thanet and Canterbury. In 1643 the County Committee fixed its headquarters at Knole, the sequestrated estate of the earl of Dorset. Towards the end of 1644 it moved to the Friars at Aylesford, perhaps because it was more centrally situated than Knole, and in 1646 it moved again, into Maidstone. At first the members of the Committee were country gentlemen who, as Deputy Lieutenants and Justices of the Peace, had been the rulers of the county before the war began. They included such men as Sir Edward Boys of Nonington, Sir William Mann of Canterbury, Sir Thomas Walsingham of Rochester, Sir Edward Scott of Scott's Hall, Sir John Honywood of Elmstead, Sir James Oxinden of Deane, Sir Edward Monins of Waldershare, Sir Edward Hales of Tenterden and Sir Thomas Godfrey of Heppington, none of whom could possibly be accused of being fanatical. However, the chairman of the Committee, Sir Anthony Weldon of Swanscombe, and owner of Rochester

95 *Knole Park*

96 *Sir James Oxinden of Deane*

Castle, was a man of different stamp, vain and ambitious, indulgent to his friends and merciless to those whom he conceived to be his enemies. Unfortunately his overbearing behaviour estranged him from many of his Kentish neighbours and now he took the frequent opportunities that were offered him, with his new power, of paying off old scores. He was supported by men like Sir Michael Livesey, known as 'the plunder-master of Kent', and Sir William Springate who was so violent in his Puritan principles that even his fellow committee-men looked upon him as mad. Gradually this group of extremists gained control of the Committee, the moderate men were excluded, and their places were taken by men who indeed belonged to the gentry but not to important county families. They were men whose names were scarcely known outside their own neighbourhood.

It was a tactical mistake to alienate, on political or personal grounds, so many of the county gentry, for only through them could the county be effectively and quietly governed. The rising of 1648 was the price that the County Committee paid for its clumsiness.

The rising can be said to have had its origin in Canterbury on Christmas Day, 1647. In June parliament had ordained that Christmas festivities were illegal, and a week before Christmas the mayor issued a warning to the citizens reminding them that no church services were to be held on 25 December, that there must be no festivities, no making of 'plum pottage or nativity pies', no hanging of holly, rosemary or bay at the street-door, and that the shops must open. The ordinance was disobeyed; a service was held at St Andrew's church and some shopkeepers refused to open their shops for trade. The mayor went about the city trying to persuade the tradesmen to obey the ordinance, but fair words gave place to invective, invective to blows, and soon there was a riot, with the mayor flung into the gutter. In the confusion a Puritan fanatic shot and killed one of the opposing party. The mayor took himself off and for some weeks the mob was in control of the city. Like all mobs, it behaved with violence, houses were broken into, and no doubt many old grudges were re-paid. That no more serious damage was done was largely due to the restraining influence of Sir William Mann and Francis Lovelace (both of whom were afterwards imprisoned in Leeds Castle for their pains). Towards the end of January a force of some 3,000 Parliamentarians recaptured the town, breaking down the city gates and demolishing part of the walls.

In May 1648 a special court sat at Canterbury to try the rioters. The Grand Jury had been carefully selected, but even so, to the keen displeasure of the judges, it refused to find a true bill, so that the prosecution could not proceed, although the accused men continued, illegally, to be detained in prison. The country gentlemen who formed the Grand Jury, Parliamentarians though they were, resolved to use this opportunity to organise a petition. In content and in style it was moderate, its main request being that people should 'for the future be governed and judged by (the English subjects' undoubted birth-right) the known and established laws of this Kingdom'. The framers of the petition intended to collect signatures to it and carry it up to parliament at the end of the month. When this news came to the ears of the County Committee, as it quickly did, the Committee expressed its 'utter detestation of such seditious practices' and forbade the petitioners to proceed with their plan.

This, for the 'Knights, Clergy and Freeholders of the County of Kent' was the last straw. A general rising took place and in their manifesto issued on 23 May the insurgents complained especially of the County Committee who 'shew their endeavour, in any cause whatever which suit not with their temper, to overrule the judgements of other persons; and meeting with opposition think they have sufficient reason to destroy the lives and fortunes (or both) of their opposers'. In truth the insurgents were not so much pro-Charles or even anti-Parliament as anti-Committee.

There were simultaneous risings in different parts of the county. The castles at Upnor, Walmer, Deal, Sandown and Sandgate were taken, and the insurgents seized the magazines of arms at Rochester, Sittingbourne, Faversham and Sandwich. Canterbury and Ashford declared for the king. Men were enlisted at Gravesend, Rochester, Ashford and Wye. Bands of men assembled under their leaders on Coxheath and on Barham Downs. Some of the leaders met to concert their plans in the house of young Edward Hales, at Tunstall, but from the beginning to the end the rising showed on the Royalist side lack of generalship and of anything in the shape of a master-plan. The fleet lying in the Downs off Deal revolted and if the seamen had had a leader capable of co-operating with the Kentish insurgents the rising might have taken a different turn. There was some talk of rescuing the king from captivity in Carisbrooke Castle in the Isle of Wight, but it came to nothing and the fleet withdrew to Holland.

97 *Sir Thomas Twisden, a lawyer who kept his head*

By the end of May the insurgents were believed to have 10,000 men under arms. Negotiations took place between them and parliament, with the Earl of Thanet as intermediary. Again the Royalists expressed their fear of the County Committee whom they accused of an 'enraged design of engaging this County in blood and ruin, when they find never so small a diminution of their arbitrary power, so long exercised over us'. But the negotiation failed, for neither side felt able to trust the other, and parliament gave the Lord General, Fairfax, authority to 'manage the business in Kent'.

Fairfax advanced from London to Blackheath, with 7,000 trained soldiers of the New Model Army, on 30 May. He divided his force into three columns, one of which marched off through the Weald to relieve Dover Castle which was besieged by some of the Royalists who had assembled at Barham Downs under their leaders Colonel Hammon and Colonel Hatton. A second column, after a sharp skirmish at Northfleet, advanced towards Rochester but, hearing that the city was stoutly defended, turned aside to Malling to rejoin the third column under Fairfax himself.

Meanwhile, on 1 June, the main Royalist forces assembled at Penenden Heath with the jovial but not noticeably competent, earl of Norwich as their general. Norwich seems to have had no idea that Fairfax was anywhere in the neighbourhood until someone with a telescope spied the Parliamentarian army. He promptly sent 1,000 men to guard the river crossing at Aylesford and threw 3,000 men into Maidstone to defend the town and the bridge. The rest of his

98 *Sir   Algernon Sidney, born Penshurst 1622, executed 1683*

men he withdrew to the high gound at Kits Coty. Fairfax, however, did not attempt to cross the river either at Aylesford or at Maidstone, but moved across Barming Heath from Malling, took Farleigh Bridge without much fighting and pressed on towards Maidstone through Tovil. The nearer he got to the town the stiffer the resistance became. His soldiers fought their way up Gabriel's Hill, which was barricaded at several points, and defended by a battery of four guns mounted at the cross-roads at the top of the hill. 'Every object in the town was got by inches' as a Parliamentarian afterwards reported. Slowly the Royalists were forced to give ground, until at midnight the last of them surrendered in St Faith's churchyard.

Norwich retreated from Kits Coty to Rochester and then pressed on to Greenwich, where he expected to meet men from Surrey and Essex who, it was understood, would rise in support of the Kentishmen. However, none joined them from the other counties and Norwich led his thousand or so men (the others by this time having deserted) across the river into Essex, where they were later to be found forming part of the garrison of the beleagured town of Colchester.

In east Kent the insurgents under Sir Richard Hardres gave up the siege of Dover Castle when the Parliamentary army appeared, and Hardres and Colonel Barkstead, the Parliamentary leader, quickly agreed upon the terms on which the insurgents should surrender. Walmer, Deal and Sandown Castles, all occupied by the Royalists, held out for some weeks. None was heavily garrisoned—Walmer, for example, was defended by 60 men. From time to time attempts were made to relieve them from the sea and several Royalist landings were made, but every time they were defeated by Fairfax's soldiers. Finally, Walmer Castle surrendered on 12 July, Deal on 25 August, and Sandown on 5 September. So ended the Kentish rising of 1648, a rising which, with good generalship and co-ordination with the fleet and with other counties, might have compelled parliament to mitigate the intolerance and the harshness of the methods of its government.

Inevitably sequestrations followed the unsuccessful rising. Men were encouraged to inform against their neighbours and again there were opportunities for working off old spites and grudges. The execution of the king in January 1649 (in which two Maidstone men were concerned, Andrew Broughton, an attorney of Earl Street, who acted as Clerk of the Court which sentenced the king, and Thomas Trapham, a surgeon, who embalmed the body after the execution) and the fanatical excesses of Cromwell's Parliament, were little calculated to win over the affection and support of the country. For the last 12 years of the Interregnum Kent had no individual history, but this was not an occasion on which it was possible to say 'Happy is the county that has no history'. For most men they were years to be endured with patience and a vague hope of better days to come. When, on 25 May 1660, Charles II landed at Dover his return was almost universally welcomed; however this, the third Stuart to sit on the throne of England, might govern his country, things could scarcely be as bad in Church or State, so it seemed, as they had been under Parliament, Cromwell and the Major-generals.

14

Kentish Agriculture from the 16th to the 19th Century

At the end of Chapter Seven on the estates of Christ Church Priory, we saw that by the 16th century agriculture had regained a good deal of its former prosperity. This chapter begins with the 16th century, where Chapter Seven broke off, and gives a survey of Kentish agriculture during the following 300 years. Throughout that period agriculture remained the most important of the county's industries, but it was carried on, as it still is, in several thousand units differing greatly in size and in efficiency. Changes in crop-rotation, in methods of cultivation and in farm machinery might take several generations to pass from the most progressive to the most backward farm. Moreover, farms vary even more according to the nature of the soil than according to the technical skill of the farmer, and Kent has such a variety of geological formations that even today there is less uniformity about farming than about any other industry. In the history of agriculture, to every general trend that can be recorded there must have been numerous exceptions.

Food-production is the main purpose of agriculture, and as a background to the history of these three centuries it is well to remember how much the demand for food was increasing—in other words, how fast the population was increasing. The figure for England and Wales in 1600 was probably about 4¾ million; by 1700 it was about a million more and by 1750 it had reached about 6¼. This was quite a slow rate of growth—half a million increase each 50 years—but between 1750 and 1800 the population increased by nearly three million, and between 1800 and 1850 it doubled, from 9 millions to 18 millions. By bringing wood- and waste-land into use the total area of agricultural land was somewhat enlarged, but the increase was small compared with the growing number of mouths to be fed. The additional demand was met partly by importing food and partly by improved farming and marketing methods. The extent of the changes which took place between the middle of the 18th century and the middle of the 19th—the period sometimes referred to as the Industrial Revolution—would almost justify the title of the Agricultural Revolution. One of the phenomena of this 'Revolution' was the number of books that were written about agriculture at the time, and much of this chapter is based upon information given in two well-known works: Boys' *General View of the Agriculture of the County of Kent* (1796 and 1805) and *Marshall's Rural*

99 *Hawkenbury Farm, Staplehurst*

100 *William Lambarde*

Economy of ... Kent, Surrey, Sussex, etc. (1798), as well as one less well known: A *Synopsis of Husbandry, being Cursory Observations in the Several Branches of Rural Œconomy*, by John Banister, gent., of Horton Kirby (published in 1799, but probably written ten or twenty years earlier).

But before coming to Boys, Marshall and Banister, we must see what was being written about Kentish agriculture two hundred years earlier by Lambarde and by Camden. Lambarde, writting in 1570, says:

> The Soile is for the most part bountifull, consisting indifferently of arable, pasture, meadow and wood-land, howbeit of these, wood occupieth the greatest portion even till this day, except it bee towards the East, which coast is more champaigne [i.e. open] than the residue.
>
> It hath Corne and Graine, common with other Shyres of the Realme: as Wheat, Rye, Barly or

Oats, in good plenty ... Neither wanteth Kent such sorts of pulce, as the rest of the Realme yieldeth, namely beanes, peason, tares ... The pasture and meadow is not onely sufficient in proportion to the quantitie of the country itselfe for breeding, but is comparable in fertilitie also to any other that is neare it, in so muche that it gayneth by feeding.

In fertile and fruitfull woodes and trees this country is most floryshing also whether you respecte the maste of oke, beeche and chesten for cattail: or the fruit of aples, peares, cherries and ploumes for men ... as for orchards of aples, and gardeins of cheries, and those of the most exquisite and delicious kindes that can be, no part of the Realme (that I know) hath them, either in such quantite and number, or with such arte and industrie set and planted ...

Touching domesticall cattel, as horses, mares, oxen, kine and sheepe, Kent differeth not much from others: onely this it challengeth as singular, that it bringeth forth the largest of stature in eche kinde of them.

Camden, who lived about the same time as Lambarde, also comments on the prosperity of the county: 'Almost the whole county abounds with meadows, pastures and cornfields, is wonderfully fruitful in apples, and also cherries.' Lambarde's reference to Kentish cattle of all kinds shows that pastoral as well as arable farming was economically important (incidentally the statement that 'Kent differeth not much from others' shows that little progress had been made, by the 16th century, towards breeding types of cattle and sheep particularly fitted to regional conditions), and Camden also refers to the 'herds of cattle' that were sent from the remotest parts of England to be fattened on the pastures of Romney Marsh—not only horned cattle but tens of thousands of sheep as well. Sheppey, too ('sheep-isle') was renowned for its sheep-rearing marshes.The general picture of a prosperous agriculture which Lambarde and Camden both paint is a true one. Other contemporary writers mention, as an illustration of prosperity, the number of new farmhouses that were being built and the number of houses that had chimneys; previously, in all except the larger houses, there had been no chimney, but only a hole in the roof out of which the smoke found its way. Other evidence that agriculture was flourishing was the number of books written on the subject. Markham, an indefatigable author (or plagiarist) published *The Inrichment of the Weald of Kent* in 1631, and *The Perfect Plat of a Hop-garden*, written by Reginald Scot, a man of Kent, first published in 1574, went into a second edition in 1576.

101 *16th- and 17th-century chimneys*

It might have been expected that the custom of Gavelkind, whereby all the sons equally inherited their father's land instead of the eldest being the sole heir, would have militated against a prosperous agriculture by fragmenting holdings into units too small to be economic. In other countries partible inheritance has created peasant farming, as for example in some regions of Germany, where there was a proverb 'Many heirs make small portions', and in parts of Ireland, where similar tenurial customs have left their mark on the face of the countryside. But Gavelkind seems not to have had this effect in Kent, for a number of reasons. First, it applied only to socage lands, and in the many large estates held by other tenures, such as knight-service or serjeanty, the rule of primogeniture operated. Secondly, a good many large landowners, especially in the 15th and 16th centuries, procured Acts of Parliament disgavelling their lands. Thirdly, if land was inherited by two or more brothers they sometimes arranged that one would buy out the interests of the others or that he would farm it out on behalf of them all; in either case the holding was not broken up. Finally, the statistical chances were against a man being survived by two or more sons of an age to inherit his land, even though by the custom of Gavelkind an heir reached majority at the age of fifteen.*

In practice therefore Gavelkind seems not to have had the disadvantageous effects on Kentish agriculture that might have been expected. On the positive side, there were a number of factors that made for agricultural prosperity. Generally the soil is fertile and the climate is favourable. Another important factor was that the open-field system of the Midlands, under which a man's holding lay in separate strips in different fields, never prevailed here.† Under the open-field or champion system each man had to go at the same pace, and follow the same methods, as the rest of the village. Experiment was difficult, the go-ahead farmer was penalised, and everyone wasted time in getting from one part of his holding to another. Kent was a county of 'enclosures', each holding forming a compact

* It is thought that the population of England may have doubled between 1100 and 1500, that is, in approximately 14 generations. This rate of growth would require a reproduction rate of 1.05 children surviving to maturity and themselves becoming parents. As about half the children would have been girls, a family with two or more grown-up sons would be the exception rather than the rule.

† This is true, broadly speaking, but there is evidence that an open-field system existed in a few places in the county.

area in which the farmer could introduce new methods and new crops as he
pleased, without seeking the approval of his neighbours. Moreover, he knew that
if he manured his land he would still be in possession of the same land in two,
three or five years' time, so that he would benefit from the expense and trouble.
Comparing them with the 'open' counties, Thomas Tusser wrote in 1573 'enclosed'
counties:

> More profit is quieter found
> (Where pastures in several be)
> Of one silly [i.e. simple] acre of ground
> Than champion maketh of three.
>
> More plenty of mutton and beef,
> Corn, butter and cheese of the best,
> More wealth anywhere, to be brief,
> More people, more handsome and pressed.

Kent was not a county of great land-owners, once the monasteries had been
dissolved and their estates broken up. The typical farm was perhaps a couple
of hundred acres in extent, and the typical farmer the yeoman who owned the
land which he cultivated. In such circumstances, there was nothing to discourage
the progressive man from planting an apple or cherry orchard, or a hop-garden.
'Hops, reformation, bays and beer' according to the old rhyme 'Came into
England all in one year'. The statement is not accurate, but it is quite likely
that the Flemish immigrants who brought with them the art of bays-making
also introduced the cultivation of the hop. It has flourished in this county since
the 16th century usually to the profit, but sometimes to the exasperation, of
generations of Kentish growers.

Hops are amongst the crops that are grown not for consumption by the
farmer and his family, but for sale off the farm for cash. In Elizabethan and
Stuart England cash-cropping was the exception rather than the rule, but in
Kent it was a more common practice than in most counties. That was because
of the proximity of London and the market which it offered for the agricultural
produce of the Home Counties. London was already eight times the size of
York, the next most important town, and was called by a contemporary writer
'the great mouth': Lambarde refers to the extent to which the county was
beholden for its prosperity to the nearness of the 'populous city' and its ready
means of transport by road and by water. As, however, we shall see in Chapter
Sixteen, by no means the whole of the county was well served for roads.

A century later the hop-gardens and orchards were the features which chiefly
impressed Celia Fiennes when she made her journey into Kent in 1697. On her
way from Sittingbourne to Canterbury 'we pass by great Hop-yards on both sides
of the Road and this year was great quantetyes of that fruite here in Kent'; from
Maidstone to Rochester 'I came by a great many fine hopp-yards where they
were at work pulling the hopps', and 'from Rochester I went that night to
Gravesend which is all by the side of Cherry grounds that are of severall acres

102 *For several centuries Kent was a principal hop growing county. Now the hop gardens are fewer in number, and all over the county scenes such as this, of hop kilns in decay, or converted into desirable dwellings*

of grounds and runs quite down to the Thames' (this must have been an exaggeration by Miss Fiennes for the river is, and was, bordered by marsh) 'which is convenient for to carry the Cherries to London'. Defoe, surveying the country 20 years later than Celia Fiennes, described the districts around Maidstone and Canterbury as 'the Mother of Hop Grounds in England', and he too, referred to the export of fruit to London, from Milton Regis on the Swale 'that is to say, Apples and Cherries, which are produced in this County, more than in any County in England, especially Cherries'. Perhaps one final literary reference is permissible: Christopher Smart, the poet who was born at Shipbourne and educated at Maidstone Grammar School and who demonstrated in his work and in his life how narrow is the line that divides genius from madness, wrote a long 'Miltonic' poem on *The Hop-garden* which was inspired by Virgil's *Georgics*, but based on first-hand knowledge of hop-growing on his father's farm. This is from his account of hop-picking in the 1740s; some of the practices and customs which he describes survived until recent years:

> See! from the great metropolis they rush,
> The industrious vulgar! They, like prudent bees
> In Kent's wide garden roam, expert to crop
> The flow'ry hop, and provident to work,
> Ere winter numb their sunburnt hands, and winds
> Engaol them, murmuring in their gloomy cells ...

From these, such as appear the rest t'excel
In strength and young agility, select.
These shall support with vigour and address
The bin-man's weighty office; now extract
From the sequacious earth the pole, and now
Unmarry from the closely clinging vine ...
One thing remains unsung, a man of faith
And long experience, in whose thundring voice
Lives hoarse authority, potent to quell
The frequent frays of the tumultuous crew ...

    [Drying the hops]
On your hair-cloth, eight inches deep, nor more
Let the green hops lie lightly...
... but more it boots
That charcoal flames burn equally below...
Constant and moderate let the heat ascend;
When the fourth hour expires, with careful hand
The half-bak'd hops turn over.

    [Putting the hops into pockets]
When in the bag thy hops the rustic treads,
Let him wear heel-less sandals; nor presume
Their fragrancy bare-footed to defile.

Hop-gardens and fruit-orchards, being exotic, naturally attracted the attention of travellers and poets, but they were not the basis of the county's agricultural economy and figure less prominently in the prosaic works of Boys, Marshall and Banister, written at the end of the 18th century. Their books are indicative of the scientific interest which was now being taken in agriculture, following the experiments of Jethro Tull with his 'horse-hoeing husbandry', of 'Turnip' Townshend with new crops in Norfolk, and of Robert Bakewell of Leicestershire in stock-breeding. Boys farmed at Betteshanger in East Kent, Banister at Horton Kirby in West Kent and Marshall was a visitor with a keen and critical eye, so from their three accounts it is possible to gain a pretty complete idea of the state of agriculture in the county at the end of the century. Boys' book was first published in 1796; it went into a second edition in 1805 and the numerous differences between the two editions show how rapidly developments were taking place during the intervening years.

Wheat continued to be largely grown, as it had been in the Middle Ages and as it still is. The area under wheat varied from time to time, depending mainly on the current market price; it was at its greatest during the Napoleonic wars, when the import of foreign corn was difficult. Part of the pasture of Romney Marsh was broken up, just as it was during the last war, and Cobbett, crossing the Marsh in 1823, found the wheat growing five feet high, adding 'I never saw corn like this before'. Banister refers to the cultivation of wheat on Erith and Plumstead marshes which made such vigorous growth that it was fed 'not with sheep only and in the early part of the spring, as is the general custom in other

places, but with a promiscuous race of horses, cows, sheep and cattle of every kind'. In spite of this treatment the crop flourished.

Except in the Weald, where the soil is unsuitable, barley, too, was very generally grown, for the brewing of beer. The practice at harvest was different in West Kent from that in East Kent. In the eastern part of the county the barley was put into sheaves before it was carried, but in the west it was carried loose into the barn. Farmers in the 18th century suffered at least as seriously from bad weather as the 20th-century farmer, but one indication of differences between conditions existing then and now is that when the barley crop failed in 1782 it was the brewers who went bankrupt!

The acreage under oats increased noticeably between 1760 and 1790. 'The chief leading cause of the increased culture of this grain', wrote Banister, 'is the present luxurious stile of living, so prevalent among every rank of people, which has multiplied the number of horses in a high degree.' The horse-population of London, in particular, was increasing rapidly and, since practically all the fodder had to be imported from the surrounding countryside, the Kent farmers who sold their oats and hay to London were sure of a good price. Oats were sown, broadcast, at the rate of 3½ to 4½ bushels to the acre, barley 3 to 4 bushels to the acre, and wheat 2½ to 3 bushels to the acre, that is about two-thirds of the quantity of seed which was being used by the monks of Christ

Church Priory on their lands in the 14th century. The rate of yield seems not to have improved much in the intervening 500 years; on the monks' land, about the year 1300, a bushel of seed could be expected to give a crop of 4½ bushels of wheat, and in 1800 the average yield in Kent was thought to be about 5 or 6 bushels. However, perhaps this is not a fair comparison, because the standard of the monks' farming was above the average of their time.

Other crops were pease and beans, grown as cattle fodder; rye, again used as cattle-fodder and for straw, it never being grown in Kent, as it was in some other parts of the country, as a bread-corn; fruit and hops, about which enough has been said already; and nuts, for which Kent was—and is—famous.

The crops so far mentioned were the crops traditional to Kent. But in the latter part of the 18th century several new crops were being introduced. Townshend in Norfolk had been proving, during the 1730s and 1740s, the profitability of turnip-growing; sheep, folded on the turnips, improved the land, especially the lighter soils, and another part of the crop, harvested for winter use, enabled the farmer 'to keep more stock, to obtain more manure, to enrich the land, to increase its yield ... Farming in a circle, unlike arguing, proved a productive process'.* The turnip crop made its way into Kent. Boys says (1796): 'Thirty years ago hardly one farmer in a hundred grew any; and now there are few, especially in the upland parts, that do not grow some every year'. According to Banister, turnip-growing so revolutionised farming on the lighter soils that the value of the land had increased threefold. Here he seems to be letting his enthusiasm for a new crop run away with him; it was true that rents were going up, but there were many reasons for the upward trend, inflation amongst them. Boys estimated that the *average* rent increased from 15s. to 20s. an acre between 1796 and 1805.

Clover, sanfoin and lucerne were known in England in the 17th century, but seem not to have made much progress in Kent before the 18th. Of lucerne Banister says, 'It is not till within these thirty years that this grass has been in much repute with the farmer ... but now that its virtues are better known ... there are few farmers that do not chuse to sow some acres of it.' It was the increase in the number of horses and cattle that made it necessary for farmers to give more attention to the management of their grass. They were also finding that it paid to give more attention to the breeding of cattle, about which Kentish farmers had been casual. In the Weald, cattle of the Sussex breed were used both for the dairy and for pulling the plough. Elsewhere they were mainly Welsh cattle or home-bred 'of various sorts and shapes', although a few cows were brought from Alderney and Guernsey towards the end of the century 'for the use of the dairies of gentlemen's families', and one or two enthusiasts were introducing 'Dutch' (i.e. Friesian) cattle. A few of the larger graziers were beginning to improve the Kent or Romney Marsh sheep, which had been evolved from the East Kent breed, but a good deal remained to be done before it acquired the qualities which have since made it so popular a breed, overseas as well as in England. By modern standards, or by the standards that prevailed

*Lord Ernle, *English Farming Past and Present.*

104 *This drawing shows farming taking place right up to Canterbury City bounds, land now occupied in most towns by extensive suburbs*

in some other parts of the country, cattle-husbandry in 18th-century Kent was backward.

Two other crops to which we have become so much accustomed that it comes as a surprise to find that in the 1770s and 1780s they were regarded as a new-fangled innovation were cabbages and potatoes. To some extent cabbages had been grown on farms for feeding to cattle, and some market-gardeners raised a few, but it was the great increase in the urban demand for vegetables that caused farmers to begin the large-scale cultivation of cabbages. The same was true of potatoes; until the last twenty or thirty years of the century the potato was not esteemed a food desirable for human consumption, but, says Bannister, 'their universal and increasing consumption at the tables of every rank, together with the appropriation of them to the fattening of black cattle and swine, hath rendered the demand for them more considerable, and in consequence the price is greatly advanced; hence the farmer has been encouraged to attempt the cultivation of them in the fields'. This revolution in popular taste took place just in time; without the potato it is doubtful whether England could have fed herself during the Napoleonic war, when at times wheat could scarcely be imported.

Two crops which on the other hand were disappearing were woad and madder, both grown for use as dyes. Probably by 1800 not a single field of madder was left, although earlier it had been quite widely grown in the Faversham district, until the Faversham farmers were priced out of the London market by their Dutch rivals. The market for woad was likewise unpredictable;

105 *A Kent or Romney Marsh sheep*

in 1791 it made £23 a load, but two years later would scarcely fetch £6. No wonder farmers were turning their attention to other crops.

Parallel with these changes in crops and in animal husbandry went changes in farming methods. The importance of crop-rotation was better understood and all over the county farmers were experimenting to see which rotation suited their own land best. Consequently so many different practices were being pursued that there could not be said to be, as in some other parts of the country, a *county* system of management. On the loamy soils of East Kent a three-year rotation, barley, beans and wheat, was found to give good results, but around Maidstone a more usual rotation was turnips, barley, clover, wheat, beans and wheat. Almost everywhere it was the custom to leave the land fallow for one summer in every three, four, five, six or seven, when it would be ploughed and cross-ploughed three or four times to get rid of the weeds and to break down the great clods of clay which formed in a few years of the ordinary cultivations. However, on the rich loam around Faversham it was found that a fallow could be dispensed with at the expense of hand-weeding the crops. With broadcast sowing eradication by hand was the only possible means of dealing with weeds, and the expense was prohibitive on all but the richest lands. Hence the importance of the drill, which enabled the seed to be sown mechanically and in straight lines so that hoeing between the rows, by hand or horse, was possible. Jethro Tull invented a drill early in the 18th century. It was some time before it was perfected, but by the end of the century it was in pretty general use, and Boys could report: 'It is much to the credit of Kentish farmers, that there are not half the weeds to be seen now on the poor lands that there were twenty years ago. The good lands have always been kept very clean.'

Tull, in his enthusiasm for 'horse-hoeing husbandry', believed that, if the farmer kept his land clean, manuring was unnecessary. Kent farmers did not subscribe to this theory, and they had a reputation for their skill in the management of the dung-yard. Apart from the manure which the farm itself produced, soot, ashes and rags were brought on to the land, London offering a ready source of supply. The heavy clay lands were regularly dressed with chalk, which was exported from Gravesend and Northfleet in considerable quantities to the Whitstable and Herne Bay area, and also across the river to Essex. Many of the so-called dene-holes in West Kent are simply mines, dug as recently as the early part of the 19th century, to get chalk for dressing the land. Lime was extensively used throughout the county, and was sold by the bushel; 'but,' says Boys, 'the lime burners have their bushel measures made of basket, and these seem annually to diminish in size'. Around the coast, and especially in Thanet, the land was dressed with sea-weed, a practice that had been followed for centuries.

The characteristic farm implement of Kent was the turn-wrest plough, the most noticeable features of which were its size and weight (the main beam, of oak, was 10 ft. long, 5 ins. deep and 4 ins. broad), and the two great cartwheels on which the beam rested. But if these were its most noticeable features, its most important difference from the Midland plough was that the turn-wrest device enabled the ploughman to plough along one furrow and down the next, whereas with the fixed mould-board plough he had to plough around a central ridge; this accounts for the ridge-and-furrow appearance which is so characteristic of old arable land in the Midlands and the North, especially where it has since been put down to grass. Visitors spoke derisively of the heavy, clumsy Kentish plou,gh Marshall being particularly contemptuous of it. However, the Kentish farmers said that it suited their land better than any other type of plough; this may have been mere conservatism, but they showed a willingness to experiment in other directions, so perhaps we ought to assume that they knew their own business best. In the Weald the wheels were commonly dispensed with and the plough was drawn by a team of up to two horses and 10 oxen. Elsewhere two, three or four horses would usually suffice.

106   *Kentish plough*

Until the early part of the 19th century reaping and threshing were both generally done by hand. They were expensive operations and to reduce the cost Boys invented a threshing machine which was driven by horses and did the work more cheaply and more quickly. The latter quality proved important in one of the years of scarcity about 1800 when foreign wheat could not be brought into the country; the millers of Deal and Dover were quite out of corn and the bakers quite out of flour and bread. Boys immediately harvested and threshed some of his wheat, it was ground into flour the next night and made into bread the next day. If the threshing had had to be done by hand the good people of Deal and Dover would have gone hungry. But, as we shall see in a later chapter, the introduction of the threshing machine was one of the things that led to labour troubles in the 1830s.

In the 19th century the history of Kentish agriculture becomes part of the history of English agriculture. The depression of the 1810s and 1820s gave way to the growing prosperity of the 1830s and 1840s, and the 'high farming' of the 1850s and 1860s. Thereafter, except for dairy-farming, agriculture slumped, as the following figures for Kent demonstrate more forcibly than any words could do:

	1867 Acres	1887 Acres	1906 Acres
Corn	244,000	201,000	142,000
Clover and rotation grasses	56,000	57,000	36,000
Hops	41,000	40,000	29,000
Turnips and swedes	33,000	25,000	17,000
Permanent pasture	288,000	358,000	429,000
Number of cows	25,000	32,000	39,000
Number of sheep	1,063,000	943,000	910,000
Men employed	47,000	40,000	31,000

The reasons for the slump must be sought in the economic history of the country and are not peculiar to Kent. Nor was the 'Agricultural Revolution' of 1750-1850 by any means peculiar to Kent, but it is only by examining the farming practices of one county in some detail that the impact of the Revolution becomes apparent.

15

The 18th-Century Country House

One sign of 18th-century prosperity was the number of country houses which were built, rebuilt, or very much enlarged and improved at that time. Kent has an exceptionally large number of country houses, usually with a park, and more than fifty of them were built or substantially reconstructed between the years 1680 and 1820. Most of them still exist, although some have been accidentally destroyed, or deliberately demolished, especially in the north-west corner of the county where 20th-century development has obliterated many of the buildings surviving from earlier periods.

The two most famous houses in Kent, Knole, at Sevenoaks, and Penshurst Place were begun in the Middle Ages. Knole was built towards the end of the 15th century and considerably enlarged at the beginning of the 17th. Penshurst Place is older, dating from the middle of the 14th century. A third great house is Cobham Hall, built about 1590 and altered a good deal 80 years later.

There were other medieval houses, of more modest size: (West) Wickham Court, Hever Castle, Sutton Place (at Sutton-at-Hone), Squerryes at Westerham, and Leeds Castle, for example. There were also few large timber-framed houses, dating from the 15th or 16th entury, which could properly be called country houses, such as Gore Court (Otham), Rumwood (Langley) and Leaveland Court. Somerhill (Tonbridge), St Clere (Kemsing), Broome Park (Barham) and Chilham Castle are examples of quite large and elaborate houses which were built in the 17th century and have not undergone extensive alteration.

The 15 houses mentioned in the two preceding paragraphs certainly do not form a complete list of pre-18th century country houses but there is no question that they are greatly outnumbered by the houses that date from that century. It was the great period of country-house building, houses which were designed to make possible a conspicuously elegant way of living and to proclaim the wealth and standing of the nobility and gentry who owned them.

Their distribution throughout the county is far from uniform. Some districts were favoured and some were shunned. Several large houses were built in the villages of north-west Kent—Beckenham, Hayes, Sundridge, Footscray, Bexley, Lesnes—conveniently near London. In the eastern part of the county, in the triangle between Canterbury, Sandwich and Dover, about ten can be counted, some of them, such as Goodnestone Park and Waldershare Park, of considerable size. But apart from this East Kent group and the group in the Beckenham area

XIII *Some of the beautifully maintained timber-framed houses in Faversham, one of the Cinque Ports. This town is jealously kept, and contains countless treasures. The old abbey founded by King Stephen and his wife has, however, completely disappeared.*

XIV *Goudhurst. Here is a rare treasure, a group of weavers' houses. The looms were situated on the first floor and the weaving families occupied the ground floor. Goudhurst, in a very lovely part of the Kentish Weald, was one of the important wool towns of the county.*

XV *On the Romney Marsh. Here is a specially beautiful section of the Royal Military Canal, built early in the 19th century to permit free movement of troops and supplies in a period dominated by the threat of invasion by Napoleonic armies.*

XVI *Hythe on Christmas Day! This lovely length of beach contains much of interest. On the extreme right is a section of beach used by the Griggs, the well-known fishing family. In the distance are some of the Martello Towers, each with its muzzle-loading gun, another of the anti-Napoleonic defences, built early in the 19th century.*

only two or three of the larger 18th-century houses lie to the north of the North Downs. The flatter land between the Downs and the Thames, including the Isle of Grain, the Isle of Sheppey, and the Isle of Thanet, was not a favoured district for gentlemen's seats. Nor was Romney Marsh or the Low Weald.

It was quite different in the High Weald, especially around Cranbrook and Goudhurst, where numerous delightful 18th-century houses still exist. All the way along the northern edge of the Weald they are to be found, especially around Maidstone and on the edge of the greensand hills. Then there is the little group where the Stour breaks through the North Downs, including Eastwell, the largest park of all, reputed to be 13 miles in circumference. From one point in Eastwell Park it is possible to see right across the county, to the Thames Estuary in the north and to the coastline of Romney Marsh in the south.

Such a view, extending over a pleasant and undulating countryside, was dear to the heart of the 18th-century country gentleman and the 'prospect' was, as much as anything, the consideration that governed the choice of a site for his house. Knole, Penshurst, Cobham Hall are to be looked *at*: they are not vantage points from which to admire the view. Different people will have different opinions about which are, scenically, the most attractive parts of Kent, but no one, however prejudiced in favour of his own corner of the county, can deny that nearly all the larger 18th-century houses are sited in districts of natural beauty.

At the end of the 18th century just about half of the Kentish country houses were in the possession of families who had owned the property (not necessarily, of course, the same building) for at least two hundred years and the other half were in the hands of families who had purchased the estate in the 17th, or more probably the 18th century. In two areas there was a marked continuity of old

107 *Eastwell Park; an 18th-century mansion 'combining elegance and convenience', now demolished*

families with comparatively few newcomers: the Holmesdale, that is the valley between the North Downs and the Greensand hills, roughly from Westerham through Sevenoaks to Wrotham; and the valley of the upper Stour, from Chilham up to Hothfield and Little Chart. In mid-Kent, that is within a radius of about ten miles of Maidstone, the 'newcomers' (many of whom had been there for almost a century by 1800) outnumbered the old families, but as might be expected it was in the north-west, in the area most closely linked with London, that there was an overwhelming proportion of owners who had themselves bought the estates whereon they resided, or whose fathers had acquired them. This was predominantly the area of the 'new' families and, significantly it was an area which, with its infertile and acid commons—Hayes, Keston, Bromley, Chislehurst and Lesnes Heath—had never had any reputation as an agricultural district.

The total amount that was spent on house-building in the 18th century was enormous. Hasted, in his *History and Topographical Survey of Kent*, written about 1785-95, constantly refers to owners who have 'greatly improved the house and grounds at very considerable expense', 'rebuilt at great expense in a most stately manner', or 'erected a most costly and magnificent edifice'. At Fairlawn, near Shipbourne, one wing of the mansion was burnt down in 1739, and promptly rebuilt. Just as it was finished it was burnt down again, but this did not discourage Lord Vane from rebuilding it a second time, in 1742. Of course not all the nobility and gentry could afford to build on this scale and sometimes the opposite story had to be told; William Henden, for example, ran through the wealth that he inherited and pulled down Biddenden Place because he could not afford to live there.

This house-building activity was, in the main, a reflection of the prosperous Kentish agriculture. From the land which they themselves farmed the owners were deriving larger profits, and from the land which they let to tenant-farmers they drew increased rents. Banister, as noted in the last chapter, recorded that the rents of some lands had increased threefold between about 1760 amd 1790, and although this must have been abnormal, landlords were undoubtedly drawing a larger revenue from their tenants.

It was not agriculture, but commerce, which supplied the money for building most of the great houses of north-west Kent—Beckenham Place, Langley Park, Hayes Place, Footscray Place, Blendon Hall and Belvedere, for example. Footscray Place (now destroyed) was built by Bourchier Cleve, of London, pewterer; the Blendon Hall property went through several hands, including those of a Director of the South Sea Company; Belvedere was built by Sir Sampson Gideon whose father, also Sampson Gideon, had bought the property; the elder Gideon was a Jewish financier of Portuguese extraction who was regularly consulted by Sir Robert Walpole, the Prime Minister, and who gave the government invaluable help in managing their financial affairs. Sir Robert Walpole's son, Sir Edward, was the owner of Hayes Place which he sold to William Pitt the elder, first earl of Chatham, and Pitt lived there whilst he was Prime Minister and in later years. This is a very different sort of society from the Darells, Derings, Tokes, Tuftons, Finches and Knatchbulls, for example, families that had been settled on their estates in the Ashford area for centuries.

108 *18th-century doorway, Bradbourne*

Houses were not built to a standard design in the 18th century, yet they have distinctive characteristics, notably symmetry and proportion. Belvedere, The Mote at Maidstone, Finchcocks at Goudhurst and Waldershare Park are typical in their balance and symmetry; the main entrance is in the centre of the front of the house and the façade to the left of the front door is matched exactly by the façade to the right. The chimney stacks are symmetrically arranged. If, as at Mersham-le-Hatch, there is a separate building, technically a pavilion, to one side of the main house and linked to it by a covered passage, it is balanced by an exactly similar pavilion on the other side. Eighteenth-century houses usually consist of a basement which cannot be seen from the park, and three storeys. The ground floor rooms are high-pitched and have tall windows; the first floor, containing the principal bedrooms, is lower-pitched and has windows of the same width as those on the ground floor but not so tall; the second floor, with the servants' bedrooms, is low-pitched and has smaller windows. This may not have been very agreeable for the servants but it gives the 18th-century house a more pleasing elevation than the modern building with windows of the same size on every floor. The elegance of proportion, the symmetry, and the orderliness of a house like Linton Place, Bourne Park, Olantigh, Chilston Park or Calehill

109 *Waldershare Park, built in the 18th century by Sir Henry Furnese*

set them apart from such picturesque and romantic houses as Knole, Ightham Mote, Sissinghurst or Gore Court.

The usual building material in the early part of the century was brick, and the mellow red brick of Bradbourne, at East Malling, or Waldershare Park is nowadays much admired. But brick became unfashionable during the course of the century, and those who could afford to do so built in stone, as the Earl of Thanet rebuilt Hothfield Place in Portland stone about 1760-70. Other buildings, constructed of brick, were given the appearance of stone by being covered with stucco.

A few houses did not conform to the usual style at all. At Mereworth Lord Westmorland, in the 1730s, built a house (misleadingly referred to as a 'castle') which has large porticos on all four sides and is surmounted by a dome. It was copied from a villa at Vicenza designed by the Italian Palladio in the 16th century. Young English noblemen and gentlemen who made the grand tour naturally visited Italy and came back with new ideas about architecture. When Bourchier Cleve built Footscray Place a generation later he, in turn, copied Lord Westmorland's Palladian villa at Mereworth.

All these houses can be said to be in the 'classical' style. The romantic movement set in towards the end of the century. Lee House at Ickham, afterwards

110 *Mereworth Castle. This building was never a castle, but a private house in the then new Palladian style, the architect being Colen Campbell. To provide the space for it, the old village and church were demolished and a new village and church built a mile away*

known as Lee Priory (it was a more romantic name but it was no more a priory than Lord Westmorland's Palladian villa was a castle) was described by Hasted as 'the most perfect style of *gothic* taste'. Hadlow Castle (another misnomer), built in the first half of the 19th century, was even more picturesque with its Gothic windows, battlements, pinnacles, minarets, and 150-ft.-high tower. At Kingsgate, Lord Holland, who made a fortune out of politics by becoming Paymaster-general, built a house overlooking the bay in the hope that the sea-air would restore his health. The tonic virtues of the seaside were just coming to be recognised at this time. He developed his estate as a remarkable mixture of 'classical' and 'romantic'. The house itself (now much altered) was supposed to represent Cicero's villa on the coast of Italy and was quite 'classical' in design but Lord Holland introduced a grotesque 'romantic' element by building in the grounds of his house a collection of follies—ruined castles, towers, refuges for hermits and the like.

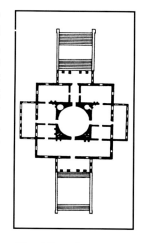

111   *Plan of Mereworth Castle*

The 18th-century country gentleman concerned himself as much about his grounds as he did about his house. Parks were laid out, trees were planted in strategic points to give a vista, streams were dammed up to form lakes, earth was moved to form hillocks and valleys. Two hundred years later it gives the appearance of being the work of nature, but in reality it was the work of landscape architects who had the imagination to foresee how their parks and grounds would look, not next year or the year after, but in a hundred years' time. The greatest of the landscape architects was 'Capability' Brown, so called from his habit when called upon for advice on landscaping a park of remarking 'I see capability of great improvement here'. He is credited with designing the grounds of several houses in Kent, including the park of Leeds Castle.

The stables often received the same careful attention as the mansion and the park. His horses were the pride and joy of the 18th-century gentleman. The stable-block was usually designed with considerable elegance, and the horses lived at least as comfortably as the grooms who looked after them.

Comfort, however, at least if measured by 20th-century standards, was not a feature of 18th-century country house life. Elegance and beauty do not necessarily go with ease and convenience. A meagre water supply and inadequate sanitation, rooms that in the winter it was impossible to keep warm, long draughty passages, the domestic quarters underground or in the attic, the kitchen perhaps 50 yards from the dining room, vast quantities of wood and coal consumed smokily and inefficiently—all these were the disagreeable accompaniments of the gracefulness and felicity of style of the great country house.

As for the kind of life that went on in this setting, Fielding has left us the picture of Squire Western in *Tom Jones*, hard-riding, hard-drinking, with no cultivated tastes, and Jane Austen (who spent a good deal of time with her brother, the owner of Godmersham Park) has left us quite another picture in her novels of a life which was genteelly conventional. No doubt both pictures are true; there were Mr. Westons as well as Squire Westerns.

One pastime which became increasingly popular amongst the country gentry, especially in Kent, was cricket. It began as a village game, probably in the 16th century, but by the 18th it had been taken up by the nobility and gentry. Like

112 *Hadlow Castle,*
c.*1840*

hunting it provided opportunity for active exercise (it was played in shoes, without pads) and like prize-fighting or horse-racing it provided opportunity for gambling. Many of the country gentlemen had their own teams, partly amateur partly professional, and would challenge each other. Sir Horace Mann, when he lived at Bourne Park, would lead his team on to the field in a match on which the stakes were as high as 500 or 1,000 guineas. He brought Aylward, one of the outstanding batsmen of the day, from Hambledon to be his bailiff, an office which unfortunately required different qualities from those of a batsman. By the early 19th century Mann was bankrupt. The Duke of Dorset at Knole was another who persuaded promising bowlers to come and work on his estate as game-keepers or gardeners. Cricket brought together the aristocracy and their tenants and servants in a common interest, and even with a touch of egalitarianism. When Kent beat an All-England eleven in 1743 by one wicket, a son of the Duke of Dorset was playing for the winning team, but he was not the captain; the captain was Val Romney, a gardener at Knole. If there had been a similar relationship between the French *noblesse* and their peasants, it has been suggested, the French Revolution would not have taken the form that it did. That is one of the might-have-beens of history, but the fact that the farmer and agricultural labourer of the 18th century shared the interests of their betters in sports and pastimes, most of them much more brutal than cricket, certainly helped to create links between social classes and to reduce the risk of violent revolution; and when finally there were outbreaks of violence, as in 1830, both sides showed a great deal of forbearance and good sense.

16

Road and River Transport

Lambarde, it will be remembered, referred to the ease of communication between Kent and London. Nevertheless, the roads of Kent were notorious for their deficiencies, and were unfavourably commented upon by numerous travellers in the county. One of the earliest Acts of Parliament to deal with roads, passed in the year 1523, describes a road in Cranbrook Hundred as 'right deep and noyous', and Celia Fiennes says of a road near Tunbridge Wells that it was 'but a sad deep unpassable road when much raine has fallen'. These statements can be quite easily reconciled with Lambarde's; until Macadam and Telford at the end of the 18th century showed how roads should be constructed with a proper foundation and with a hard surface, they were simply unsurfaced tracks. Whether they were good or bad depended almost entirely upon the nature of the soil, and upon the weather. So the roads on the Wealden clay were impassable for wheeled traffic during much of the winter, although they were tolerable during the summer and autumn, whereas the roads on chalk and gravel could be used thoroughout the year. Watling Street could thus be reckoned a good road throughout much of its length, running as it mainly does along the foot of the dip slope of the chalk of the North Downs.

Until only 150 years ago, the villages of the Weald were sometimes almost cut off from contact with the outside world for several months in the year. Most of the roads were originally drove-ways, for moving cattle to and from the upland manors to the Wealden pastures and feeding-grounds. In consequence, most of the more important roads in the Weald still run roughly north and south. The 'repair' of the Wealden roads at the end of the 18th century is described by Hasted, who says that the highway from Tenterden to Ashford was scarcely passable after rain, the horses plunging into the mud up to the girth of the saddle, and the waggons sliding along on their hubs; he adds 'the roads were of fifty to sixty feet wide with a breadth of green sward on each side; hedges filled with oak trees overhanging the road with stone causeways for foot passengers. When they became dry in the summer they were ploughed up and laid in a half circle to dry, the only amendment they ever had'. Oxen with their cloven hooves, were better fitted than horses to the pulling of carts and carriages on roads like this, and it is not surprising that pack-horses, which could use the narrow stone causeway at the side of the road, were generally employed to move merchandise in the Weald.

113 *The Pantiles, Tunbridge Wells*

135

Conditions were made even worse by the dragging of timber from the Wealden forest down to the river at Yalding where it could be sent off to Chatham and London, and by the carrying of heavy loads of iron from the furnaces at Lamberhurst, Brenchley, Cowden and elsewhere. A statute of Queen Elizabeth's reign required that any iron-master carrying charcoal, ore or iron for a mile on any highway between 12 October and 1 May should likewise carry a cartload of cinder, gravel, stone, sand or chalk for the repair of the road. It is unlikely that any great effort was made to enforce the Act, or that, in any case, this method of repair would have been effective.

The lack of any adequate system of maintaining the roads was the root of the trouble. The main bridges (except Rochester Bridge) were the responsibility of the county, the procedure being for the Justices of the Peace to arrange with a contractor for necessary repairs to be done and for a rate to be raised to meet the cost of the work. Maidstone, Farleigh, Yalding, Tonbridge, Lamberhurst and Wye bridges were amongst the seventeen or so maintained in this way (Wye Bridge still bears an inscription that it was built in 1638 at the charge of the county of Kent and repaired at the same charge in 1684). Rochester Bridge is exceptional, in that it has been maintained, for at least the last 600 years, out of the income from extensive estates owned by the Bridge Wardens. All the more important bridges were therefore effectively looked after.

The roads, on the other hand, were the responsibility not of the county but of each parish through which they ran—and Kent has over 400 parishes. Every parishioner was obliged to work on the roads for a certain number of days in

114 *East Farleigh bridge*

each year, or to provide materials for mending them, or to lend a cart and horses. The work was supposed to be supervised by a Highway Surveyor, chosen each year from amongst the parishioners. The Surveyor did not stay on the job long enough to learn much about the technicalities of road-repairing, the unpaid labour was unwillingly given, and no parish was likely to bother about maintaining its roads at a higher standard than its own parochial needs demanded; if one of the roads which crossed the parish happened to be the main road from London to Rye or from Rochester to Canterbury, why should the unfortunate parishioners be expected to go out of their way to keep it up better, and at greater cost, than the rest of their roads?

115 *The medieval seal of Rochester Bridge Wardens*

The parochial system obviously would not serve for the main roads especially with the increase in traffic towards the end of the 17th and during the 18th century. This increase was due to the rising standard of living, to the increase of population, and to the growth of towns, especially London, which gave a stimulus to commerce. Under Cromwell, an attempt was made to appoint a 'Minister of Roads' and to institute a system of road maintenance for the whole country, but it was two or three hundred years before its time, and it failed. The device which Parliament hit upon, towards the end of the 17th century, was to empower a body of men to undertake the maintenance of a length of road, and to charge a toll for its use—the turnpike system. The first two Kentish Turnpike Acts were passed in 1709 amd 1711, one for 'repairing and amending the highways leading from Seven Oaks to Woods Gate [Pembury], and Tunbridge Wells', and the other for 'Amending and Maintaining the Road between North-fleet, Gravesend and Rochester'. Both of these roads were extensively used, the Gravesend to Rochester road by travellers who came by the long ferry from London to Gravesend as the first stage of their journey, and the Sevenoaks to Tunbridge Wells road because it was part of the main road from London to Hastings and Rye, and also because of the traffic going to the 'Wells', which by the end of the 17th century had become a highly fashionable resort. Another reason for taking this road in hand was that between Sevenoaks and Tonbridge it ran across the Wealden clay, and was undoubtedly 'a sad deep unpassable road' after heavy rain.

By the middle of the 18th century many other stretches of road had been turnpiked, including those from Rochester to Canterbury, from Rochester to Maidstone, from Canterbury to Whitstable, from Dartford to Northfleet, from Pembury to Flimwell, from Farnborough to Sevenoaks, from Footscray to Wrotham Heath and from Maidstone to Cranbrook. Many of these are quite short stretches of road; there was no idea of treating, for example, the London to Canterbury, the London to Hastings or the London to Folkestone road as a whole, and turnpiking it from end to end. The turnpike trustees were usually local gentlemen who put up the money for their local roads mainly from a sense of public duty; few of them expected to get a good return on their money, and sometimes they were lucky to get any at all. The turnpike trusts performed a public service, often clumsily, sometimes inefficiently, occasionally corruptly, no doubt, at a time when there was no public authority able to undertake the proper upkeep of the roads.

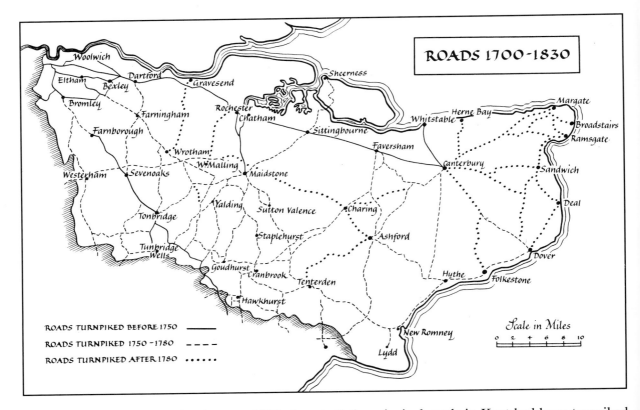

116 *Map showing the development of the turnpike system in Kent*

By the year 1800 almost all the principal roads in Kent had been turnpiked (see the map above) although those from Canterbury to Sandwich and Deal, and from Sandwich to Dover were not dealt with until just after the turn of the century, and a few others were later still; the Gravesend to Wrotham road was turnpiked under an Act passed as late as 1825. Even so some of the cross turnpike roads in the Weald were still 'as bad as can be imagined; being even impassable for coaches or chaises very frequently in winter'. Apart from the fundamental difficulty that these roads ran over clay, the tolls collected were insufficient to enable the trustees to purchase, and bring from a considerable distance, the stone and other materials required for the constant repairs. The turnpiking of a road did not relieve the parishioners of their duty to give a certain number of days maintenance work each year, but in the Weald it was materials rather than labour that presented the difficulty.

In a century, the roads of Kent had undergone a reformation. However, it was not until the 1820s and 1830s that Macadam's ideas about roadmaking became generally accepted and that roads were constructed with a hard, rolled, stone surface (not of course, *tar* macadamised at that time), although almost to the end of the 19th century a few of the by-ways were still 'soft' unmetalled roads, that lay inches deep in dust during the summer, and even deeper in mud during the winter. In many parts of the county there was a sudden improvement in the condition of the roads during the years immediately following the Napoleonic war. A large number of men were unemployed, and the Overseers of the Poor turned them to work on the roads. It was even said that you could judge the proportion of unemployed in a parish by the condition of its roads.

The farmers of Kent were by no means pleased to see road improvements being carried out in other parts of the country. They feared, and rightly, that an efficient highway system would give the more distant counties access to the London markets, and that the near-monopoly of the Home Counties would be broken down. According to Adam Smith it was this fear of competition that caused Kent and other neighbouring counties actually to petition Parliament against the extension of turnpike roads to the remoter counties. This attempt at protectionism came to nothing, but it shows that the farmers of Kent had a clear understanding of the commercial importance of the new turnpike roads.

Water-borne transport played an extensive part in the commerce of the 18th century, the great era of canal construction. Canals are most numerous in the Midlands, and South Lancashire and Yorkshire, the districts which were becoming rapidly industrialised. Only one canal was built in Kent (apart from the Royal Military Canal, which was part of the Napoleonic war defences), linking the Thames at Gravesend with the Medway at Rochester. Its construction was expensive, because it involved building a two-mile-long tunnel between Higham and Strood, through the spur of chalk that runs out into the Hundred of Hoo. The distance from Gravesend to Strood is seven miles, and as the alternative route round by the Nore is about fifty miles, the canal might have been expected to prove a paying proposition. In fact, it did not. The canal, although it was begun in the early 1800s, was not opened until 1824. It was soon seen to be a failure, and twenty years later was bought by the Railway Company who ran their line from Gravesend to Strood through the tunnel. Although it has nothing to do with canals, we might mention here another

117 *A stage-coach*

unsuccessful venture, to construct a road tunnel under the Thames from Gravesend to Tilbury. It was originally estimated to cost £12,853 8s. Work was begun in 1800, and when it came to an end three years later all that had been achieved was a shaft at Gravesend, 85 ft. deep and full of water, which had cost £15,242 10s. 4½d. The 19th century was full of examples of enthusiasm outstripping engineering skill and financial prudence.

One of the engineers who was consulted, late in the day and inconclusively, about the Gravesend tunnel project was John Rennie, the celebrated builder of London, Waterloo and Southwark Bridges and of the London Docks. At about the same time he was preparing a scheme for a canal in the Weald to link the Medway with the Rother, with branches running to Lamberhurst, to Hever, and to Wye. Such a scheme was too ambitious to gain support, but in 1812 an Act of Parliament was passed for constructing a canal from the Medway, at Brandbridges, to join the Royal Military Canal at Appledore. However, in this case financial discretion prevailed, and the project was never attempted.

But although the canal schemes failed, Kent was certainly not without water-transport. Dartford and Gravesend on the Thames, Milton Regis and Faversham on the Swale, and Rochester and Maidstone on the Medway, all did a considerable amount of trade, especially with London. Smaller places on the Medway, like Snodland, New Hythe, Mill Hall, Aylesford and Yalding also had their wharfs where barges could be loaded and unloaded, and some boats even got as far up as Tonbridge. The Stour was navigable by barges as far as

118 *A riverside wharf at Maidstone. From the wharves would be shipped large quantities of stone from local quarries, corn and other produce of the Weald, timber and sand*

119 *River-traffic at Gravesend*

Fordwich, and from there to Canterbury the road was good. For coastwise shipping there was Ramsgate Harbour, completed in the 1760s, Sandwich Haven, navigable by small ships, Dover Harbour, reconstructed about 1750, and Folkestone Harbour, built about 1810. With these coastal harbours, the county was fairly well served for water-borne transport.

The busiest riverside town was undoubtedly Gravesend. It was closely connected with the East India trade, and it was the usual practice for ships to take on board their final provisions there, before starting on a long voyage. With the construction of the London Docks between 1802 and 1828, this part of the town's trade fell away. The 'long ferry' traffic, however, continued undiminished up to the middle of the century. In 1816 there were 26 sailing boats, of from 22 to 45 tons, plying daily between Gravesend and London. The first steam-boat ran in 1815, but it was constantly breaking down—the longest period of continuous service that it ever gave was three weeks; the next year it was sold for use on the Seine, where one can only hope, for the reputation of the country of its manufacture, that it proved less temperamental. However, other and more reliable steam-boats became available, and the traffic steadily increased. By 1833, 290,000 passengers were being carried annually, and ten years later the number of passengers embarking or landing at Gravesend exceeded 1,000,000 a year, a volume of traffic that must have taxed the two piers to their capacity. Forty-four omnibuses met the boats, running regularly to Rochester, Chatham, Maidstone and elsewhere. But the coming of the railway in the middle of the century saw the end of Gravesend's busy-ness.

17

Village Life in the Early 19th Century

The war against Revolutionary and Napoleonic France went on for over twenty years. Its effect on the nation's economy was little understood at the time. Because more money was in circulation in 1815 than in 1793 there were many people who believed that, as a result of the war, the wealth of the country had increased. Hard experience gave the ordinary farm worker a truer understanding of the situation; his wages went up, but prices went up even more, so that he was poorer in 1815 than in 1793, not wealthier. In this chapter we shall see something of the events that rural poverty led to in Kent.

The rapid growth in the population which began about the middle of the 18th century continued throughout the 19th. It was caused not so much by an increase in the birth-rate as by a reduction in the death-rate, for reasons which are not yet fully understood, but probably included a better diet for most people and some improvement in medical practices. In 1801, for the first time an

120 *Biddenden village*

official census was held and it has since been taken every 10 years (except in 1941). The earlier census figures are not altogether trustworthy and, moreover, the statistics for a parish may be distorted by the presence, for example, of a work-house, a lunatic asylum, or a barracks, or a large number of labourers building a railway line in the neighbourhood. The figures must therefore be used with caution, but they are, of course, much more reliable than such unofficial estimates of the population as were made in earlier centuries.

In almost all the villages in Kent the population continued to increase steadily and sometimes rapidly up to the middle of the century. Thereafter, the increase continued in those villages which became industrialised (e.g. Horton Kirby, Cliffe, Higham, Halling, Snodland, Aylesford and Burham) or which were so near a town as to come under its influence (e.g. Charlton-next-Dover, Hoo St Werburgh, Bearsted and Hackington). Elsewhere the tendency was for village populations to begin to diminish after the 1850s and 1860s, often falling by the end of the century to a lower figure than that returned in the first census. The following figures are typical of villages which were not affected by industrial development or close urban contact:

121 *Sowing in the early 19th century*

	1801	1821	1841	1861	1881	1901	1921
Waltham	383	582	544	608	506	360	313
Stodmarsh	110	122	145	145	134	75	109
Boughton Malherbe	327	475	512	408	445	380	366
Frinsted	153	152	202	219	208	126	150
Hollingbourne	730	1,000	1,300	1,190	1,151	945	754
Hunton	583	683	740	935	870	821	780
Mereworth	597	711	862	835	843	717	684
Luddesdown	172	235	275	279	268	240	212
Biddenden	1,151	1,544	1,486	1,412	1,352	1,058	1,120
High Halden	519	724	683	653	637	507	632
Smarden	831	1,038	1,141	1,130	1,139	994	992
Newnham	262	356	455	409	312	301	299
Godmersham	337	414	450	388	358	336	233
Benenden	1,300	1,746	1,594	1,662	1,598	1,336	1,308
Ridley	47	74	95	101	65	64	73

The trend shown by these figures, that is a rapid increase to a peak about the middle of the century and then a fall continuing into the 20th century, is especially noticeable of the villages in East Kent; it is generally less true of those in the western part of the Weald; and in West and North Kent, the area of industrial and urban development, the population increased steadily throughout the century (see map on page 144).

A few villages had a local industry, such as stone or chalk quarrying or brick-making, but the staple industry which sustained village life was agriculture. Banister, Boys and Cobbett, from their different points of view, have a good deal to say about the conditions of the agricultural worker in Kent during the 40 years from the 1780s to the 1820s. Banister turned a farmer's jaundiced eye upon farm workers who '(being of a race the most low bred and illiterate) do often turn out the most unprincipled and profligate; and though perhaps they

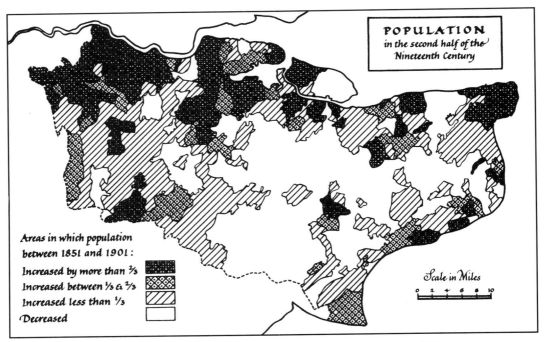

POPULATION
in the second half of the Nineteenth Century

Areas in which population
between 1851 and 1901:

Increased by more than ⅔
Increased between ⅓ & ⅔
Increased less than ⅓
Decreased

Scale in Miles
0 2 4 6 8 10

122   *Map showing the population of Kent in the second half of the 19th century*

123   *Map showing the population of Kent in the first half of the 20th century*

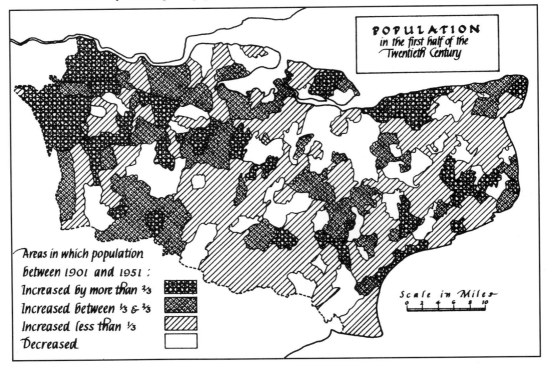

POPULATION
in the first half of the Twentieth Century

Areas in which population
between 1901 and 1951:

Increased by more than ⅔
Increased between ⅓ & ⅔
Increased less than ⅓
Decreased

Scale in Miles
0 2 4 6 8 10

may not have attempted the commission of the most atrocious offences, yet in the low arts of deception, the country ploughman is inferior to few'. Boys deals with the subject of farm labour more coolly, although he urges that piece-work rather than day-work rates should be adopted wherever possible, adding 'When a number of labourers work together by the day, much time is lost by idle conversation'. He also says that farm labourers were more difficult to get along the coast (other occupations being open to them) than in the interior of the county. In other counties, such as Lancashire and Yorkshire, the development of industry opened up other fields of employment, men left the land to work in the towns, and the shortage of labour caused agricultural wages to rise. This was not generally true of Kent where there was very little industrial development until the latter part of the 19th century. Such shortage of labour as existed here was due to the Army's demand for men during the French war. Between 1770 and 1798 farm wages in Kent nearly doubled, fell sharply after the Treaty of Amiens in 1802, began to rise again when the war was resumed in 1803 and by 1815 were at least double the wages of 1793. However, during that same period prices of food had trebled.

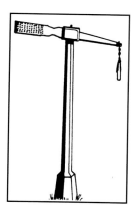

124 *A rural pastime: the quintain, Offham*

A social change was also taking place in the relationship of the farmer to his servants. Up to the last quarter of the 18th century the unmarried farm servants, men and women, actually lived under the farmer's roof (or the roof of one of his outhouses) and had their meals, cooked by the farmer's wife, in her kitchen. On the larger farms there would probably be as many as 10 or 12 servants living in and, however uncomfortable such an arrangement may have been to both sides, it certainly meant that the farmer and his wife were in close contact with their labourers. But farmers were going up in the world, farmers' wives wanted their kitchens to themselves, and by the end of the 18th century the custom of living-in was going out of favour all over Kent. Of course it did not disappear suddenly, and even in 1850, when there were over 4,600 farms in the county, the number of men living in still averaged slightly over one per farm.

In East Kent around the year 1800, a waggoner or ploughman could expect to earn £12-£15 a year and his board. A plough-boy or a dairy-maid would receive about £4-£7 a year with board, and a cook £4-£8. A married day-labourer, living in a cottage for which he paid £2 or £3 a year, would earn 2s. to 2s. 6d. for a 10-hour day, and a shepherd about the same. Married labourers could usually buy pork and wheat from the farmer at reduced prices. The price of bread varied a good deal according to the harvest: a quartern loaf might be anything from 5d. to 8d. Potatoes cost about 10s. for a 200-lb sack, and meat 8d. to 10d. a lb. Certain jobs, such as threshing, were done as piece-work and gave the farm-worker the chance of earning a much-needed few extra shillings. Hop-picking gave work for all his family, and, if he was lucky enough to be employed on hop-drying (an operation requiring great skill and allowing little chance for sleep), he might get 15s. to 25s. a week, with unlimited strong beer and spirits. The wages of a pole-puller would be about 10s. 6d. to 15s. a week which, in spite of the fact that his only allowance was of small beer, Banister regarded as 'a very good salary'.

125 *Alfred Mynn of Harrietsham: the finest mid-19th-century cricketer*

In one respect the agricultural labourers of East Kent were worse off than those employed in other parts of the county: the Weald and West Kent are in general, well-wooded, and the countryman could get his fuel cheaply by gathering it for himself out of the woods. East Kent, by contrast, is thinly wooded, so the farm worker had less chance of getting free fuel. Coal from Newcastle was imported at all the coastal and river towns, but it cost 40s. to 50s. a chaldron and was beyond the reach of the poor.

Apart from piece-work, hirings of labour were commonly by the year from September to September. Once a man had been engaged it was illegal for him to leave his employment or for anyone else to employ him during the year. Advertisements like this (from the *Kentish Gazette* for 26 January 1796], are quite frequent in the local papers of the period:

RUN AWAY

From his Master's service on Monday last, Philip Bartlett, waggoner's mate; about five feet two inches in height, dark brown hair, freckled face, and walks lame with his left leg. Had on when he went away a swanskin waistcoat and plain long trowsers.

Whoever will bring him to Mr. Daniell Bushell of Ickham shall receive Half-a-guinea reward, and all reasonable expences. Should any person employ him, they will be prosecuted as the law directs. If he will return to his Master's service immediately, he will be again received without any notice taken of this first offence.

The economic depression that followed the Napoleonic war was sharply felt in rural Kent. Cobbett, whose account of his tour through Kent in September 1823 is perhaps more lively than reliable, refers to the poverty in the eastern part of the county: 'The labourers' houses all along through this island [i.e. Thanet], beggarly in the extreme. The people dirty, poor-looking; ragged, but particularly *dirty*.' Their poverty he ascribed to the fact that so much work on the farm was now done by horses and by machines. Boys, as we have already seen, had invented a threshing machine on his farm at Betteshanger and the invention spread rapidly. Large numbers of men were without work and looked to the parish for relief. Some were employed on the roads, but they worked unwillingly and supervision was lax.

This depression and poverty formed the background to the Last Labourers' Revolt (as it has been called by the Hammonds) which broke out at Hardres on the last Sunday in August 1830, when some four hundred labourers destroyed a number of threshing machines. Throughout the month of September risings continued around Canterbury and more threshing machines were destroyed. By October the trouble had spread to the Dover district. The ricks of unpopular farmers were burnt, and others received threatening letters signed 'Swing'. In spite of their lawless behaviour, the rioters attracted a good deal of sympathy, even amongst the county gentry and landowners. Their grinding poverty was undeniable, and it was not only the farm-workers who looked with disfavour upon new-fangled contraptions, like threshing machines, which took away men's work. Seven trouble-makers who were tried at the East Kent Quarter Sessions in October were let off with a nominal sentence of three days' imprisonment. In spite of—or perhaps because of—the leniency shown by Quarter Sessions, riots broke out in other parts of the county, especially around Maidstone and Sittingbourne, the men demanding regular work and wages of half-a-crown a day (the comparative wealth of Kent is shown by the fact that when the rising later spread to Hampshire, Wiltshire and Berkshire the demand was only for two shillings a day, and in some parishes the labourers asked for no more than 8s. or 9s. a week).

An efficient police force would have had no difficulty in coping with the riots. But whilst London acquired an organised police force for the first time in 1829, it was to be nearly another thirty years before such a force existed in Kent (the County Constabulary was formed in 1857), and meanwhile the magistrates had either to rely on the parish constables, who were unpaid and generally incompetent, or to call in the military. That is what the Maidstone magistrates did on 30 October when they went out with a troop of soldiers to meet a mob of 400 people just outside the town. The ringleaders were arrested without difficulty, but Peel, the Home Secretary, fearing further trouble ordered two pieces of artillery to be sent to Maidstone. They were not needed; in Kent the rioters did not carry things to extremes, and generally their demand for half-a-crown a day was felt to be reasonable. When, in November and December, the disorder spread to Sussex, Hampshire, Wiltshire, Berkshire and Dorset, the riots in those counties were more violent and the punishments inflicted in the subsequent trials correspondingly more severe than in Kent.

For thirty years or so before the rising broke out the inadequacy of farm-workers' wages had, in fact, been publicly and officially admitted by the practice of making up a man's wages out of the parish poor-rate to an amount considered sufficient to keep body and soul together. In Kent the wages of a married man with three children would usually be made up to 12s. a week, with an extra 1s. 6d. a week for every child beyond the third. Thus farmers paid low wages knowing that they would be supplemented from the poor rate. The cost of supplementing inadequate wages with the cost of maintaining the increasing number of men who could not get work, resulted in rates which were so high that in 1833 a Royal Commission was set up to enquire into the administration of the Poor Law. The Report gives a good deal of evidence about conditions in Kent, as well as in the remainder of the country, carefully selected, no doubt, to support the Commissioners' recommendations for the reform of the Poor Law.

Lenham was one of the parishes which the Commissioners used to illustrate their findings. Its population had gone up from 1,434 in 1801 to 2,197 in 1831, and the amount expended on the poor from £1,468 in 1806 to £4,299 in 1832. No fewer than 1,200 of the 2,200 inhabitants were receiving some form of parish relief in 1833. The rates were so high that two tenant-farmers, unable to pay their way, had given up their farms, which the landlords could not re-let. Wages in the summer were 2s. 3d. a day, wet days excepted and rather less in winter. From November round to May the number of unemployed was

126 *Mowing, late 18th century*

60-70: 'the population of this parish', reported Mr. Majendie, 'is beyond the demand for labour'. Emigration to the colonies had been encouraged, the cost of the emigrants' passage being met by the parish, but the 50 parishioners of Lenham who had gone to Quebec found that work there was as hard to get as at home, and the letters which had been received from Canada were so unfavourable that it seemed unlikely that any more Lenham men would go to seek their fortune in North America.

By 1833 it had become uncommon in Lenham for labourers to live under their employers' roofs. They were generally considered to be less industrious than formerly (has there ever been a generation when this was not the commonly held view?) and they did not attempt to lay by anything against a rainy day. That they did not save is scarcely surprising; an industrious labourer might get £35-£40 a year and 'his wife and four children, aged 14, 11, 8 and 5 years' might expect to earn a further £3-£5 a year. On this income it was thought that a family could just about subsist, eating bread, cheese, suet-puddings, potatoes and occasionally salt pork, with tea to drink. Presumably some vegetables would be available from the cottage-garden, but subsistence for the ordinary farm labourer was at no more than peasant level. The conditions that are described in the report on Lenham were, broadly, typical of those which prevailed over the county as a whole.

In consequence of the Commissioners' Report, the Poor Law was reformed and its administration made more efficient. But its efficiency was of a mechanistic kind, and its inhuman administration was one of the causes that led to the extraordinary Courtenay rising in 1838, said to be the last occasion on which a soldier was killed in battle on English soil. The self-styled Sir William Courtenay, Knight of Malta, was an impostor, a Cornishman named Thom who deluded his followers, and probably himself, into believing that he was the Messiah. He appeared at Canterbury in September 1832, exotically garbed and claiming that he had just come from the Middle East. He stood as a candidate at the Parliamentary election in December. His appearance on the hustings dressed in what he took to be the costume appropriate to a Knight of Malta created a sensation, and although he was not returned to Parliament he succeeded in getting some 500 votes in a total poll of about 2,000. A few months later, as a witness in a lawsuit, he gave evidence which quite obviously was just story-spinning. It was not a case in which he was personally involved and he stood to gain nothing by his action. He was afterwards charged with perjury convicted and ordered to be transported, but the sentence was respited. He served a short term of imprisonment and then was moved to what was clearly the proper place for him, the lunatic asylum at Barming.

Whilst he was in the asylum Courtenay was allowed to issue manifestos to his followers in the Canterbury district, signing them as 'King of Jerusalem'. Towards the end of 1837 he was released into the keeping of a friend who lived at Boughton-under-Blean, and there he stayed until January 1838. Meanwhile his eccentricity increased, he took to carrying a brace of pistols and a sword, and he soon had a following of some hundreds of men and women whom he could work up into a frenzy of hysteria. Some followed him because they believed in

127 *Sir William Courtenay,* alias *Mad Thom*

his religious rantings, some because they were dissatisfied with their lot in life, with their low wages, and with the harshly efficient new Poor Law.

Courtenay remained in the neighbourhood of Boughton and Dunkirk during the early months of 1838, stirring up more and more trouble, until on 30 May a warrant was issued for his arrest. The brother of the constable who went to arrest him was shot by Courtenay who then withdrew with his followers into Bossenden Wood on the north side of the London Road, about a mile on the Canterbury side of Dunkirk. The magistrates sent to Canterbury for the military. When the soldiers arrived they entered the wood and, after marching for a mile and a half, came up with Courtenay. He was called upon to surrender; his answer was to shoot the lieutenant and a civilian who was standing nearby. Then the magistrates ordered the soldiers to fire, and Courtenay and half-a-dozen of his followers lay dead.

So ended the life of this unfortunate, deluded man. In itself it was an affair of little importance, but it served to draw attention to the conditions under which a great part of the rural population lived, and especially their backwardness and ignorance. It so happened that Dunkirk lay outside any parish, and therefore had no church and no parson. To this fact was ascribed the backwardness of the people, and funds were collected for building a church and appointing a vicar. The church was built in 1840 and a few years later a school was opened. Thus, indirectly, did Courtenay benefit Dunkirk, but in a manner unforeseen and unintended.

The building of public elementary schools which went on throughout the century was a reflection of the interest now being taken by the middle and

128 *The end of the Courtenay Rising, 1838*

THE TRAGIC SCENE AT BOSENDEN WOOD, NEAR CANTERBURY.

[*Drawn by an Eye-witness, expressly for the* PENNY SATIRIST.]

129 *Horsmonden School: erected in 1853 at the cost of the Rev. Sir William Smith-Marriott, Bt., and Sir John Smith, Bt., for 140 children*

130 *Horsmonden village shop*

upper classes in the moral and mental welfare of the 'labouring, manufacturing and other poorer classes'. In 1830 not more than a dozen Kentish villages possessed an elementary school (Benenden, Biddenden, Molash, Nonington, Petham, Sheldwich, Southfleet, Stelling, Ulcombe, Waldershare, Westerham (Hosey Common) and Westwell). Between 1830 and 1840 schools were built in more than a score of villages and between 1840 and 1850 nearly forty more were erected. In each of the two following decades some fifty new schools were opened, so by the date that the Elementary Education Act of 1870 became law, schools existed in more than 170 rural parishes. Most of them were Church schools, owing their origin to the enthusiasm and energy of the local rector or vicar, and sometimes also to the generosity of local landowners. A small number of schools were built by non-conformist churches and chapels, but on the whole they were more active in the towns than in the country. Attendance was not made compulsory until 1876 and as many of the earlier schools could not hold by any means all the children in the parish they had to be enlarged during the later years of the century.

The Act of 1870 enabled School Boards to be set up for parishes where the schools were insufficient, the Boards' duty being to build new schools to make good the deficiency. The immediate effect of the Act was to put the Churches on their mettle and a large number of Church schools were built in the early 1870s. The total number of Church and Board schools built in rural Kent between 1870 and 1880 was more than seventy. Indeed, by 1880, almost every village had a school of one kind or another; this is shown by the fact that between 1880 and 1900 only 17 villages acquired their first school, although in some, where the population was still growing, it was necessary to build a second, or even a third, school.

131 *British School, Snodland, 1835-90*

The building of this large number of elementary schools throughout rural Kent between 1840 and 1880 reflects not only the increased concern which was now being shown for the well-being of the poorer classes; it is also an indication of the growing prosperity of the country districts, culminating in the period of 'high farming' in the 1850s and 1860s. Although agricultural wages did not rise much, prices fell and the farm-workers were better off than ever before. Some people emigrated from their own villages, going off to the large towns, especially London, or venturing overseas, but it was found that the intensive farming which was being practised in the middle of the century gave employment to considerably more men than the Poor Law Commissioners had ever thought possible. Moreover, the railways and the improved roads meant that villages were less isolated, and they opened up some chance of employment in nearby towns, although for many purposes the village remained a self-sufficient community. If ever there was a 'golden age' of village life, perhaps it was about 1860 or 1870.

18

Urban and Railway Development in the 19th Century

We have seen how, in the rural parts of Kent, the population increased until the middle of the 19th century and then often began gradually to decline. In the towns, on the other hand, and in the villages which grew into towns, the increase of population continued throughout the century and indeed has continued to the present day, except in the old-established Wealden market towns such as Cranbrook and Tenterden, where the population has remained more or less stationary (in number) for the last hundred years.

Apart from the general growth of population, the main causes of urban development in 19th-century Kent were: the industrialisation of Thames-side, of the lower Medway Valley and to a less extent of Swaleside; the construction of the railways, and consequently the close linking of West Kent with London; and the emergence of the seaside holiday custom.

Towards the end of the 18th century Canterbury was still the largest town in the county, with a population of over 9,000, followed by Rochester and Maidstone, each with about 8,000 inhabitants, and Dover with rather more than 7,000. By 1801 Chatham had outstripped Canterbury, the census figure being 10,500 which no doubt included many sailors' and soldiers' families living in the town, busy at that time with naval and military preparations for the French war. For much of the 19th century Chatham remained the most populous town in the county, although later it was surpassed by its neighbour, Gillingham.

By 1800 Margate and Ramsgate had established themselves as seaside resorts, followed by Broadstairs, Deal, Dover and Folkestone. Sea-bathing and the drinking of sea water, as an alternative to visiting the well-known spas, began to come into fashion soon after the year 1750. The Royal Sea Bathing Hospital at Margate was founded in 1791, by which time the town's reputation as a seaside resort had already been established for 30 or 40 years. The visitors usually came from London by boat. Charles Lamb, in an essay written in the 1820s, remembered with affection 'the most agreeable holyday of my life' which he spent at Margate in 1790 and the journey thither from London in 'the old Margate hoy'. The first steam-boats, of about 70-80 tons, began to run about 1815, and when they got over their teething troubles made the trip more quickly and with considerably more certainty than the sailing ships which might take anything from 8 to 40 hours. Nevertheless, even by steam it was

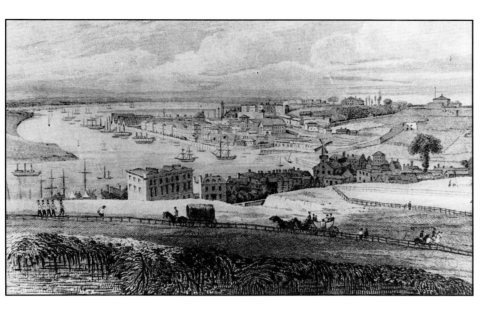

132 *The view over Chatham Docks*

a lengthy journey, and the latter part of it in open water with no protection from the Essex coast. Some few passengers were bold enough to risk the discomfort of rounding the North Foreland and made for Ramsgate (as salubrious as Margate and rather more select), but most of the Ramsgate visitors came overland from Margate. Throughout the 19th century the two resorts were in rivalry, with Ramsgate (including St Lawrence) leading in population except for the first 20 years or so, as these figures show:

	1801	1821	1841	1861	1881	1901	1921
Margate	4,800	7,800	11,000	10,000	18,200	26,700	46,500
Ramsgate	4,200	7,600	13,500	15,100	23,100	28,400	37,200

(The census in 1841 and again in 1921, was taken in June at the beginning of the holiday season, and the figures for those years must have included a fair number of visitors.) Some of the most attractive urban architecture in Thanet, e.g. Cecil and Hawley Squares at Margate, and Wellington Crescent, the Paragon, and Royal Crescent at Ramsgate, belongs to the period when the two towns were developing into thriving and fashionable resorts. From the harbours of both towns, Ramsgate's dating from the 18th and Margate's from the early 19th century, packet-boats plied regularly across the Channel to Boulogne and Ostend.

Broadstairs enjoyed something of the reflected glory of its two larger neighbours. For those who preferred a more genteel, quieter holiday, with everything on a miniature scale, Broadstairs possessed great attraction and it grew steadily from being a somewhat scattered township of less than 1,600 souls in 1801 into a flourishing resort with a population of over 7,000 in 1901; and during the last 150 years, like its expansive neighbours, it has continued to grow.

133 *The resort of Margate in the 1920s*

Herne Bay, on the northern coast of the county, developed at much the same rate as Broadstairs. Deal was already a town of some size by 1800 and did a lively trade, lawful or otherwise, with the many ships that anchored in The Downs to avoid bad weather or to await a favourable wind. After steam had ousted sail The Downs were less used as a safe anchorage, and the resultant decline in Deal's commerce was scarcely balanced by its development as a resort. Indeed, the population figure for 1841, when the census was taken in the holiday month of June, was actually a little below the figures for 1811, 1821 and 1831, when the count was made in May. From 1800 to 1900 Deal just about doubled its population, a much slower rate of growth than that of the Thanet towns.

Dover was primarily a port for passage to and from the Continent, and a garrison town; it was only secondarily a seaside resort and probably it owed its development as such to the large number of visitors, mainly military with their ladies, who frequented the town at the time of the French war. In the 1830s and 1840s it was a fashionable rather than a popular resort, and Marine Parade and Waterloo Terrace stand (or did, until some years ago) as reminders of 19th-century Dover as a watering-place of *ton*.

Like Dover, Folkestone, as a seaside resort, dates from the time of the French war when soldiers were encamped in the neighbourhood, and the town, along with its neighbours, Sandgate and Hythe, flourished as it had never done before.

However, when the war came to an end Folkestone made little headway. Its population, which numbered 4,200 in 1811, rose to 4,500 in 1821, fell to 4,300 in 1831, rose to 4,400 in 1841—and by 1851 was 7,550. Thereafter the town prospered, its population reaching more than 30,000 by the end of the century. This comparative newness of Folkestone is strikingly illustrated in its buildings; outside the old town, down in the ravine towards the harbour, it is almost impossible to find a building of anything but Victorian, or later, architecture.

Folkestone's sudden boom was due to the building of the South Eastern Railway from London, which was begun in 1842 and reached the coast in 1843. It was not the first railway to be constructed in Kent. The earliest, which was also the first railway to be constructed anywhere in the world to convey passengers by locomotive, was the six-mile line from Canterbury to Whitstable, opened on 3 May 1830. Although Canterbury was still the premier town in the county, the more far-sighted citizens saw that it was bound to be outstripped by other towns with better means of transport, and a scheme was mooted for making the Stour navigable as far up as Canterbury. An Act of Parliament was obtained in 1825 authorising the scheme, but it was found to be too costly and, as an alternative, a harbour was constructed at Whitstable and linked with Canterbury by a railway line. The land between the two towns rises to a height of 200 ft. and the railway involved a tunnel half a mile in length and banks with gradients of 1 in 40 and, in one place, 1 in 28. Stationary engines were installed to pull the trains up the steeper slopes. The locomotive, the *Invicta*, proved less powerful than had been hoped and its use had to be confined to a level stretch of the line hardly more than a mile in length. In fact, the *Invicta* so disappointed the Railway Company that they offered her for sale in 1839, but no purchaser could be found. Now she stands by the Dane John garden in Canterbury and probably few people who see her realise that she was the first locomotive ever to haul (although only just) a passenger train. The line continued in use for a century, and with the packet boat that sailed every other day from Whitstable for London formed for some years the speediest and easiest route between Canterbury and the capital.

The Canterbury and Whitstable Railway is not to be compared in importance with the South Eastern Railway, running through Tonbridge and Ashford to Folkestone and Dover. In the early days of railways. Parliament was determined to see that the country was not unnecessarily 'cut up' with lines, and there was to be only one outlet from London to the south and the south-east. The South Eastern were therefore compelled to run over, first, part of the London and Greenwich Railway, next over the Croydon Railway, and then over the Brighton Railway before striking off eastwards at Redhill on to its own line. One advantage of the route which it followed through the Weald was that the line could be laid out almost dead straight for the whole 46 miles from Redhill to Ashford, and there were few gradients to be negotiated. The disadvantage of this route was that it ran through the less populous parts of the county and missed the developing towns in the north, and in the Medway Valley. When in 1845-6 the South Eastern Company put forward projects for new lines to serve the centre and north of the county they hinted that they had been obliged to adopt the

134 *The opening of the Canterbury to Whitstable railway, 3 May 1830*

135 *The locomotive,* Invicta

Tonbridge-Ashford line because of opposition of landowners and towns (especially Maidstone) elsewhere. No doubt there was some truth in the allegation, but it did not weigh sufficiently with Parliament to enable the South Eastern to get the additional powers that they were seeking.

A primary reason for carrying the South Eastern line to the coast was to attract the cross-Channel traffic. The continuation of the line from Folkestone to Dover, which involved building the 100-ft. high Foord viaduct at Folkestone, and four tunnels and a sea-wall along the coast, as well as blowing up part of the cliff, was a major engineering feat. The opening of the line in 1844 made it possible to complete the journey from the French or Belgian coast to London comfortably within a day.

136 *The Foord viaduct, Folkestone*

Maidstone's first line, opened in 1844, ran along the Medway from Paddock Wood (then known as Maidstone Road). It soon took away the traffic from the Maidstone coaches, although the distance to London by rail through Paddock Wood, Tonbridge and Redhill was 56 miles, as against 35 miles by road.

The next year a branch line was constructed from Tonbridge to Tunbridge Wells, which had been known as a fashionable spa since the 17th century. As with every other town in West Kent, a railway link with London immediately led to rapid expansion; the population of the parish of Tonbridge which, in the 19th century, included also Tunbridge Wells, went up from 12,500 in 1841 to 21,000 in 1861 and 29,800 in 1871.

There was an equally striking growth in the size of Ashford immediately after the railway works were built there. In 1841 Ashford and Willesborough together had 3,700 inhabitants. In 1851, two years after the works had opened, the number was 6,000 and 10 years later, 7,700.

In 1846 the South Eastern built a line from the main line at Ashford, following the Stour Valley to Canterbury and a year later extended it to Ramsgate and Margate, with a branch from Minster to Sandwich and Deal. Thus the Thanet resorts obtained a railway link with London, but by a long and circuitous route, and the railway did not bring about a development at Margate and Ramsgate comparable with that at Folkestone.

In the northern part of the county the first line to be built was the London and Greenwich Railway, opened in 1836, which was constructed throughout its whole length of three and three quarter miles on a viaduct of brick arches. Another line in North Kent was laid a few years later, from Gravesend to Strood, alongside the canal; in the tunnel it was, apparently, laid on the canal towpath. Opened in 1845, it was purchased during the following year by the South Eastern Company who filled up the canal through the tunnel, and laid a double track. Its westward extension, the North Kent Railway from Gravesend *via* Dartford and Charlton to join the London-Greenwich line, was constructed in 1849. Seven years later a railway was built following the west bank of the Medway, from Strood to Maidstone, connecting there with the line to Paddock Wood.

137 *The entrance to S.E. Railway Works, Ashford*

Up to the middle of the century the South Eastern had virtually a monopoly of railway transport in Kent. In 1853 a new company, the East Kent Railway, obtained powers to construct a line from Strood *via* Chatham, Sittingbourne,

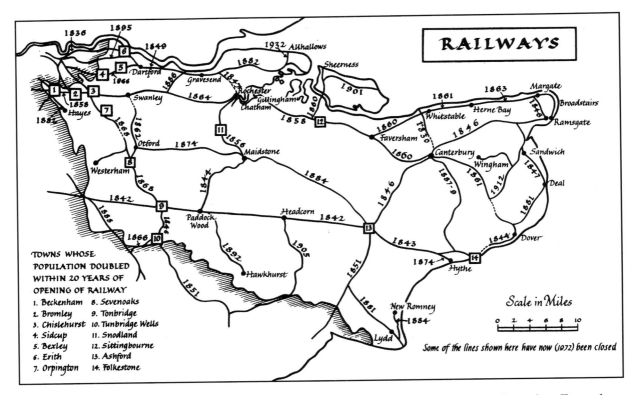

138 *Railways in Kent*

and Faversham to Canterbury. When it was opened from Strood to Faversham in 1858, and to Canterbury in 1860, it seemed a harmless little local line unable to compete with the South Eastern system. However, a period of sharp rivalry opened up when the East Kent Company (and their subsidiary) were granted wider powers, and extended their line both eastward and westward—from Canterbury to Dover (1861); from Faversham to Whitstable (1860); Herne Bay (1861), and Margate and Ramsgate (1863); and from Rochester across the Medway *via* Sutton-at-Hone (now Swanley Junction) to St Mary Cray (1861), whence the East Kent (afterwards more suitably known as the London, Chatham and Dover) had running rights over the lines of other companies to London. With these extensions the 'East Kent' ceased to be an unimportant local line and competed directly with the South Eastern for the continental traffic at Dover, for the Thanet traffic, and for the traffic from the Medway towns. With railway transport available, Sittingbourne developed as an industrial town (its population increased by 60 per cent. in the 20 years following the opening of the railway); and a branch line was constructed to Sheerness and Queenborough, over the ill-fated Kingsferry Bridge, in 1860.

After this, the main railway development, as the map above shows, was in West Kent, which shared in London's rapid expansion. Everywhere the opening of a new line was followed by a marked increase in population:

	Railway opened	Population								
Beckenham	1858	1851	1,700	1871	6,100	1881	13,000	1901	26,300
Bromley	1858	1851	4,100	1871	10,700	1881	15,200	1901	27,400
Chislehurst	1865	1861	2,300	1871	3,300	1881	5,300	1901	7,400
Orpington	1865	1861	1,700	1871	2,400	1881	3,100	1901	4,300
Sevenoaks	1868	1861	4,700	1871	5,900	1881	8,000	1901	9,700
Bexley	1866	1861	4,900	1871	6,400	1881	8,800	1901	12,900
Sidcup	1866	1861	300	1871	400	1881	1,900	1901	5,800

The development of these towns occurred, in the main, because the railway made it possible for thousands of men and women to work in London and share in its growing prosperity, whilst living in Kent. Along Thames-side, from Gravesend westward to the London border at Woolwich, the expansion was partly due to the railway link with London, and partly to industrial development. No place exemplifies the extent and character of the change on Thames-side more vividly than Erith. In 1841 its population was 2,082, and that included 221 harvest labourers, the census having been taken on 7 June; 10 years later it was scarcely larger; in 1861, however, it was 4,100, in 1871 8,300 and by 1901 over 25,000. Crayford doubled, and Dartford trebled, in size between 1861 and the end of the century. A similar development overtook the villages between Dartford and Gravesend, as these figures show:

	Stone	Swanscombe	Northfleet
1861	1,000	2,300	5,700
1881	2,500	4,500	8,800
1901	5,100	7,000	12,900

In the last thirty years of the century the railways and industrial development shifted Kent's centre of gravity, economically and in terms of population, from the east and south to the north and west. So long as Kent was primarily an agricultural county, the poorer lands in the north-west did not count for much; as industry grew and the county became increasingly under the influence of London, so the formerly undeveloped north-west took on a new importance. Penge, Beckenham, Bromley, Orpington, Chislehurst, Sidcup, Bexley, Erith, Crayford and Dartford, in area a twentieth of the whole county, now contain over one-third of the total population; a century ago the population of the same area represented scarcely more than a twentieth of that of the whole county.

139 *Victorian Tudor station, Aylesford*

The shift in the centre of gravity is reflected in the Parliamentary representation. Before the Reform Act of 1832 not a single borough west of the Medway returned a member to Parliament; today (if the Rochester and Maidstone constituencies are omitted as belonging to mid-Kent) West Kent returns eight members against six from East Kent. The representation of Kent in Parliament before 1832 reflected in a rough and ready way the balance of importance as it had existed in the Middle Ages. The county itself was represented by two Knights of the Shire; Canterbury, Rochester, Maidstone and Queenborough

140 *Crayford Town Hall, once Vickers canteen*

each returned two members, and so did the Kentish Cinque Ports, Dover, Hythe, Sandwich and New Romney. In all, therefore, Kent sent 18 members to Parliament.

In some of the boroughs the elections were comparatively democratic even before the Reform Act. At Canterbury, for example, there were 1,000 voters and no one exerted an undue influence on them. Maidstone had 600 voters and, although earlier in the 18th century the town's two seats were regarded as being at the disposal of the earl of Aylesford, his influence had declined. Rochester had the same number of voters, namely, 600, but one of the two seats there was customarily filled on the nomination of the Board of Admiralty, or of Ordnance, that is, the Government of the day. The Government always managed to secure the election of its nominees at Queenborough where the number of voters was 131, of whom 56 were employees of the Admiralty or the Ordnance. There were many Government employees also at Dover, but as the total number of electors for the borough was 1,200, the Government could not often command more than one of the two seats. Sandwich with 480 voters, was much under the influence of the Government and so was Hythe. The number of electors at Hythe was 126, all of them freemen of the borough, but only 22 of them resident in the town. The other 104 were scattered all over the country, and probably most of them never visited the town except to cast their votes. The situation at Romney was even more scandalous for there were only eight electors, all tenants of Sir Edward Dering, and all voting for the candidates of their landlord's choice. It was the most flagrant example of a 'nomination borough' in the county.

The Reform Act of 1832 did not alter the number of members of Parliament for the county as a whole, but some seats were redistributed. Queenborough and New Romney ceased to be represented and Hythe's representation was reduced to one. Sandwich kept its two members, but the constituency was enlarged to include Deal and Walmer. Chatham was given one seat, and Greenwich (then part of Kent) was given two. Finally the number of County members was doubled, East Kent and West Kent each returning two. The distribution of Parliamentary seats was thus brought more nearly into line with the distribution of population and wealth in the county. However, the rapid growth of some towns during the 19th and early 20th centuries as a result of industrial development and proximity to London has made necessary several subsequent redistributions of seats since the great Reform Act of 1832.

19

Industrial Development in the 19th and 20th Centuries

At the beginning of the 19th century Kent was predominantly an agricultural county, with few other industries and those mainly small. The dockyards at Chatham (where the *Victory* was built) and Sheerness were the largest industrial centres, and even there it was alleged that the number of employees was kept at an unnecessarily high level in order to provide support for Government candidates at elections. Paper-making was carried on in a small way at Maidstone, Crayford, the Crays, Eynsford, Buckland, Crabble and two or three other places. Whitstable had a works, dismal in appearance, for making copperas, a substance used in dyeing and tanning, the raw material of which was a certain kind of pebble found locally and in Sheppey. There were salt-works at Stonar and in the Isle of Grain. From Pitcher's yards at Northfleet ships of up to 1,000 tons and even beyond were regularly launched. Brewing and brick- and tile-making were carried on in all parts of the county, and quarrying wherever there was chalk or stone. But, apart from the dockyards, all these industries were on a small scale.

In 1834 William Aspdin began at Northfleet to make Portland cement, so called because it was thought to resemble Portland stone. Its manufacture required chalk and clay, and since both of these were found in the neighbourhood, whilst the river was available to transport the finished product, Thames-side was an obvious area for the development of the industry. It was the cement industry which largely accounted for the rapid growth of Northfleet, Swanscombe and Stone, to which reference was made in the last chapter. Later in the century cement-making spread to the Medway Valley between Upnor and Burham, leaving as its legacy great scars in the North Downs where chalk has been quarried, and industrial villages such as Eccles and Wouldham. Its effect on the villages of the Medway Valley is shown by the census figures: in the 20 years between 1861 and 1881 the populations of Burnham and Halling almost doubled and of Snodland and Wouldham almost trebled. From agricultural villages they grew, within a generation, into industrial townships. The cement works of the Medway Valley depended mainly on barge-transport and therefore were handicapped in competition with the Thames-side works which were accessible to larger ships. In consequence the cement industry along the Medway came nearly to a standstill in the slump of the early 1920s, but since then the

141 *H.M.S.* Victory, *built at Chatham*

development of road transport has resulted in a revival of cement-making on the west bank of the river; on the east bank the abandoned factories have crumbled into picturesque ruins. Fortunately the large paper-mills of Messrs A. E. Reed and Co. Ltd at New Hythe, which were begun in the early 1920s, expanded rapidly and gave employment to some of the men who were thrown out of work by the contraction of the cement industry in the Medway Valley.

The first expansion of the paper-making industry followed the abolition, in 1861, of the excise duty on paper. The Dartford Paper Mills, on the River Darent, were erected in 1862. At the end of the century the introduction of the halfpenny newspaper and the popular magazine resulted in a further increased demand for paper and again the industry expanded. Apart from the mills at New Hythe the industry has developed on a large scale at Dartford, Northfleet and Sittingbourne. All three places are conveniently situated for the import by water from the Baltic and from Canada of logs and wood-pulp, the most important raw materials, and for despatching the finished product to London, the great paper-consuming centre.

At Dartford engineering has been an industry of growing importance for the last century. Erith owed its rapid expansion to the establishment there in 1889 of the Maxim Nordenfelt Gun and Ammunition Company, a concern which was taken over by Vickers in 1898 and to the development of Frazer and Chalmers' engineering works. The opening of Vickers' factory at Crayford during the 1914-18 war resulted in the town doubling its size in the course of a few years. The industrialisation of the Thames-side area has been carried further in the present century by the establishment of cable and electrical equipment works at Erith and Northfleet, of chemical works at Dartford, and of a large electricity generating station at Littlebrook. From Gravesend westward the whole of Thames-side has become an industrial area interspersed only by marshes and worked-out chalk pits.

Throughout the 19th century and until recent years Chatham dockyard has constituted the largest industrial centre in the Medway towns, but engineering is also an important local industry, and so was the building of flying boats until Shorts' works were moved to Belfast in 1946. At Maidstone industrial expansion—motor-engineering and the manufacture of foodstuffs—dates only from the 1890s and 1900s, although here as elsewhere in the county (notably at Faversham) the brewing industry has a much longer history. At Sheerness, as at Chatham, the dockyard was the main industry until its closure some years ago, but during the last sixty years or so the glassworks at Queenborough have provided employment for a considerable part of the local population. Sittingbourne owes its industrialisation to the paper-mills, established about 1840 and much enlarged since the 1914-18 war, and to brick-making, an industry which expanded rapidly during the 19th century to meet the growing demand for bricks, especially from London. Bricks are bulky and heavy to move and the availability of water-transport and of brick-earth is sufficient to account for this industry's flourishing at Sittingbourne.

Lying between the industrialised areas of Thames-side and the Medway towns are the Hundred of Hoo and the Isle of Grain which for long remained wholly agricultural, except for a cement works and an explosives factory at

143 *The Medway Brewery, Maidstone*

144 *Dover ferry port*

Cliffe. However, in the 1920s an oil storage plant and refinery were established at Grain and since then they have grown into a gigantic installation, again, like many other industries in Kent, making extensive use of water-transport.

The presence of coal in East Kent had been suspected for many years before it was proved in 1891 by borings made from the abandoned workings for the projected Channel tunnel. At Tilmanstone and Snowdown coal began to be mined just before the 1914-18 war, at at Chislet in 1918. Betteshanger pit was some ten years later. For some years inadequate means of transport handicapped the Kent coal industry. The East Kent Light Railway, winding its way from Shepherdswell through Eythorne and Tilmanstone to Eastry, where one line branched westward to Wingham and the other north-eastward to the (1914-18) war-time port of Richborough, was constructed to serve the coal-field, but did not prove very successful. In 1930 an aerial ropeway was built to convey coal from Tilmanstone to Dover Harbour, a distance of six or seven miles but that, too is now disused. For the accommodation of miners and their families who came to Kent from all over the United Kingdom new townships were established at Aylesham, Elvington and Hersden. The new industry has made its mark upon on the landscape and upon social conditions in East Kent, but in neither respect perhaps has its effect been so devastating as was feared

145 *The considerable coal reserves under Kent were thought capable of profitable mining. This is Tilmanstone mine, one of several to be built. All the mines in Kent have since been abandoned*

146 *The development of atomic power—the power station at Dungeness, on the south coast of Kent*

(or sometimes hoped) sixty or seventy years ago, and Chislet is now closed. Even more conspicuous than the colliery pit-head gear are the huge electricity generating stations at Richborough and Dungeness, which dwarf everything else in the landscape.

During the last few years new industries have grown up, but, except for a few districts such as Richborough and the Cray Valley around St Paul's Cray and St Mary Cray, they are generally distributed widely over the county rather than concentrated into new industrial areas. Almost entirely, they are light industries with relatively easy problems of transport. The development of the motor-lorry and the motor-bus in the last sixty or seventy years and more recently the universality of the motor-car have linked together town and country for work, for shopping, for sport and for entertainment. By the 1960s few villages were without a bus service, even those where, seventy years earlier, the carrier's van, going once or twice a week to the nearest market town, was almost the only link with the outside world. Scarcely noticed, Kent passed through a transport and a social revolution in little more than a generation.

The most remarkable development in this area is, of course, the construction of the Channel Tunnel between Folkestone and Calais. The project took seven years to realise, at a cost of £6 billion plus interest, and was officially opened by HM Queen Elizabeth II and President Mitterand on 6 May 1994. The Eurostar service, based on the French TGV, started on 14 November 1994 and allows the passenger to travel from London to Paris in three hours, while the journey to Brussels takes 15 minutes longer. These times will be reduced with the introduction of a high-speed rail link from London to Folkestone which is planned for early next century.

20

Defence against Invasion

The last two chapters have emphasised how its situation, on London's door-step, has been one of the major influences in the history of Kent. Much of the 19th- and 20th-century urbanisation resulted from nearness to the capital. Another important factor throughout the county's history, both in peace and in war, has been its proximity, on the other side, to the Continent,

> a soil that doth advance
> Her haughty brow against the coast of France

as Wordsworth described the county in the sonnet which he addressed to the men of Kent, 'vanguard of liberty', when the fear of a French invasion was at its height in 1803. Threat of invasion has repeatedly given the county anxious and stirring times, some of which have left their permanent memento in the form of defence works. It was the risk of a French invasion that caused the fortification of Chatham Lines, begun in 1758, and when Britain was again at war with France from 1778 until 1783 Fort Amherst was built as an additional protection to the dockyard and Chatham Barracks were erected to house the garrison.

There was a far more real danger of invasion 20 years later, when Bonaparte boasted that 'with three days east wind I could repeat the exploit of William the Conqueror'. Kent made preparations for defence. In 1794 volunteer troops of horse were raised in several different parts of the county. The French army was known to march on its stomach, and therefore plans were elaborated for removing cattle and foodstuffs from the eastern, the more vulnerable side of the county, so as to deny the enemy provisions if he succeeded in making a landing. Even on paper the plans were incomplete, and whether it would have been possible for a mere handful of Volunteers to drive the cattle from East Kent into the depots which were to be arranged at Cobham and elsewhere in West Kent was a question which fortunately never had to be put to the test; the chaos that would have resulted from driving some thousands of cattle over old Rochester Bridge can be imagined, and how the livestock were to be removed from the Isle of Sheppey, whether by rafts or by a temporary bridge, seems never to have been settled. As part of the defence preparations parishes were required in 1798 to make a return of men between the ages of 15 and 60 who could help in the defence of their county; of infirm and elderly people who

147 *Grain fort: mid-19th century*

would not be able, without assistance, to remove themselves in time of invasion; and of waggons, horses, cattle, foodstuffs, etc. At Folkestone, of a total population of about 3,200, between 1,200 and 1,400 were unable to remove themselves from the district without help, 215 men were already serving as sailors, soldiers or privateers, and another 140 expressed themselves as ready to volunteer, nine as horsemen and the rest as foot-soldiers, the great majority as pikemen, not more than ten venturing to serve with firelocks. The returns for the other coastal towns, if they were available, would probably show a similar state of affairs.

More conspicuous signs of the preparations to resist the threatened invasion were the Martello towers and the Hythe Military Canal. From Copt Point, just east of Folkestone, where the high chalk cliffs come to an end, right round the more vulnerable parts of the coasts of Kent and Sussex, was built a series of small forts of the same design as the tower at Cape Martella in Corsica, which the British Navy had been given cause to respect. Many of the Martello towers still exist. They are brick-built, the walls 5 to 8 ft. thick, the diameter about 22 ft. at the top, and the height about 30 feet. Each tower was designed to house, in considerable discomfort, a garrison of 20 to 30 soldiers, and to mount a 24-pounder gun. Having, in the basement, a reservoir of water and stores of food and ammunition, a Martello tower could, so it was thought, withstand a siege. Contemporary critics disputed the effectiveness of these fortifications, but as to their costliness there could be no dispute. The main purpose of the Military Canal, which was dug along the landward side of Romney Marsh from Hythe to Rye, was to hold up the enemy if he succeeded in making a landing on the Marsh. Every quarter of a mile or so there is a break in the line

148 *Hythe's military past. Here are the old military barracks, two of its Martello towers and a section of the Royal Military Canal, which still runs through the town*

of the Canal, and at each bend an embrasure was constructed for heavy cannon. This defence work also came under criticism, and men asked scornfully whether Napoleon, who had thrown armies across most of the major rivers of Europe, was likely to be held up by this glorified ditch.

At Chatham, the defences were further strengthened by the building of Fort Delce, Fort Clarence and Fort Pitt, although the latter was not completed until some years after the war had come to an end. Whilst the risk of invasion still existed, large military camps were established at Chatham, Coxheath, Barham Downs, Brabourne Lees, Dover and

149 *A Martello tower*

Shorncliffe. On the coast vigilant watch was kept for the enemy; when the wind was fair for a crossing from France the guard was trebled and the Folkestone records show that the streets were patrolled all night.

A problem which confronted the defenders, before the day of the electric telegraph, was how to send messages from the coast to London. The old-fashioned beacon system merely enabled some sort of warning to be given, but it could not be used for transmitting anything but the simplest messages. It was to meet this need that, in 1796, a line of semaphore stations was constructed from London to the coast, the distance between the stations being six or eight miles, so that a message spelled out at one could be read by the neighbouring station and relayed along the line. A brief message, it was said, could be sent from the coast to the station at the Admiralty in London in two minutes. The line of stations in Kent was Shooter's Hill, Swanscombe, Gad's Hill, Beacon Hill (with a branch *via* Tonge and Furzehill to Sheerness), Shottenden Hill, Barham Downs, Betteshanger and Deal. Industrialisation had not yet overtaken West Kent and the Medway towns, and the atmosphere was clean enough for a system of visual messages to be feasible; today, industrial haze and smoke would too often reduce visibility to make such a system reliable.

With the Battle of Trafalgar the danger of a French invasion receded, and with the Battle of Waterloo it was removed altogether. Apart from fears which were entertained for a brief period in 1858 about the intentions of Napoleon III (it was about this time that a Martello tower was built to defend Sheerness Dockyard) the people of Britain could turn their attention for the rest of the century to the business of making money and prospering. To that era of peace and prosperity the 1914-18 war put an abrupt end. For the first time for a hundred years a British army was fighting in western Europe and Kent was on the main line of communication with the front in Flanders. Soldiers in their hundreds of thousands sailed from Folkestone Harbour, and war material was

150 Dymchurch gun

shipped across the Channel from the hurriedly constructed, and now derelict, port of Richborough. Dover, where the Admiralty Harbour had recently been completed, was the base from which the Dover Patrol operated with such dash and brilliance that its exploits have become legendary. German bombs were dropped on Kentish soil, Thanet towns were shelled by German men-of-war, and even as far inland as Maidstone the ominous and continued rumble of gunfire could be heard from the battlefields of France.

These disturbances were small compared with those of the 1939-45 war, when Kent was not on the line of communication, but was itself for years in the front line. In 1940 the danger of invasion was as acute as it had been in 1803. Along all the beaches steel scaffolding and barbed wire were put up to discourage enemy landings, guns were mounted at commanding points round the coast, anti-tank ditches were dug around the key towns, part of the civilian population was evacuated, and at strategic points pill-boxes were built which will presumably remain as a lasting reminder of Hitler's War as the Martello towers are of Napoleon's War. In the autumn of 1940 the aerial Battle of Britain was fought out largely over Kent and the Thames Estuary. There were fighter stations from Biggin Hill in the west to Manston in the east, and anti-aircraft batteries were established everywhere, even on stilt-like forts which were constructed off the north coast, out in the mouth of the river. Four years later Kent proved a convenient depository for flying bombs, destined for London, but prematurely brought down by fighter aircraft, by gunfire, or by balloon barage. In a new fashion the county was playing once again its accustomed part of vanguard in the defence of England. Happily, when hostilities were over it could still repeat, with truth its proud motto, *Invicta*.

Whether it can make the same claim in the more subtle warfare against uglification and Subtopianism is more doubtful. In the long run the face of the county has suffered more from invasion from the west than from the east. Much of the urban sprawl is inevitable, industrialisation has brought prosperity, and public authorities do their best to plan and control development; but need the 20th century be quite so careless of appearances? Wordsworth! it is *thou* that shouldst be living at this hour; we have need of thee, to urge the Men of Kent and Kentish Men of today to fresh vigilance in the face of another and less civilised enemy than the Frenchmen who vainly waited in the Channel ports nearly two hundred years ago. Only if we are vigilant whilst there is yet time, will our descendants be able to say with Michael Drayton, writing in 1613:

<blockquote>
Fair Kent
What countrie hath this isle that may compare with thee?
</blockquote>

Index